Arbeitsbuch zu

Deutsch für alle

BEGINNING COLLEGE GERMAN: A COMPREHENSIVE APPROACH

SECOND EDITION

Werner Haas

The Ohio State University

Gustave Bording Mathieu

California State University, Fullerton

John Wiley & Sons

NEW YORK   CHICHESTER   BRISBANE   TORONTO   SINGAPORE

ISBN: 0-471-86403-X

Printed in the United States of America

10 9 8 7 6

Vorwort

This workbook accompanies *Deutsch für alle*, Second Edition, a program for first-year college German. The exercises in the workbook are based on material presented in the corresponding chapter of the textbook.

Each workbook chapter consists of three parts. The first, *Selbst-Test*, is a self-testing section designed to help you review the material presented in the *Dialog* and *Grammatik* of each chapter. The answers to the questions are provided in the right-hand column, allowing you to check immediately how well you have learned this material. Place a piece of paper over the answer column, then move it down a line at a time to check your response to each new question on the left. In some cases, you may wish to write in your answer; therefore, longer than usual blanks are provided for some exercises.

The *Selbst-Test* is closely coordinated with the textbook. It begins with questions on the *Dialog*, and progresses through each section of the *Grammatik*, including the *Fehlergefahr!* feature. It offers a complete review and reinforcement of the grammar points discussed in the text. If the self-testing indicates that you need to study a grammar structure further, turn to the parallel section of the *Grammatik* in the textbook.

The second part of each workbook chapter is the *Probe-Test.* These are primarily writing exercises which review the grammatical, structural, and vocabulary materials presented in each chapter. The *Probe-Test* ends with *Erweitern Sie Ihren Wortschatz!*, which tests fifty important words and expressions introduced in the chapter. The instructor may assign and collect the *Probe-Test* as a "dry run" for tests he or she may wish to devise. The answers to the questions in the *Probe-Test* are provided in the Instructor's Manual.

The third part is an *Antwortbogen*, or answer sheet, for the *Hör' zu...und antworte* exercises of the laboratory tape program. You will need to take the *Arbeitsbuch* with you to the laboratory in order to record your responses.

Following the exercises on the eighteen chapters of the textbook is a *Review of errors often made by English-speaking students of German.* This unique section offers you an opportunity to test your ability to distinguish between more than thirty linguistic pitfalls by writing the German equivalents of the short English sentences provided.

The *Anhang* also contains the English equivalents of all the dialogs from the textbook.

The *Aussprache Übungen* in the workbook contrast German vowel sounds and consonant sounds both with each other and with English. This section is recorded on a separate reel of the laboratory tape program.

W.H.

G.B.M.

Inhaltsverzeichnis

Kapitel 1

Selbst-Test

The *Selbst-Test* section is designed to help you review and reinforce the material presented in each chapter and to show how well you have learned it. Cover the right-hand column with a piece of paper. As you finish each item, move the paper down to check the correct answer.

DIALOG

Translate the underlined expressions.

1. Wer ist sie?   — Who is she?
2. Wie geht's?   — How are you?
3. Ich spiele leider nicht sehr gut.   — unfortunately

1. Subject pronouns

4. The case of the subject is also known as the _____.   — nominative
5. The German equivalent of the English pronoun *I* (is/is not) capitalized.   — is not
6. English *you* has three equivalents in German: _____, _____, and _____.   — **du, ihr, Sie**
7. At the beginning of a sentence, **Sie** may communicate English _____, _____, _____, or _____, depending on the ending of the verb.   — *you, she, they, it*

Complete with the appropriate subject pronoun.

8. *What's your name?* (formal) Wie heißen _____?   — Sie
9. *What's your name?* (familiar) Wie heißt _____?   — du
10. *He dances well.* _____ tanzt gut.   — Er
11. *They like to play.* _____ spielen gern.   — Sie
12. *Do you like to dance, Miss Weber?* Tanzen _____ gern, Fräulein Weber?   — Sie
13. *Are they nice?* Sind _____ nett?   — sie

14. *We have no time.* _____ haben keine Zeit.　　　　— Wir
15. *I play tennis.* _____ spiele Tennis.　　　　　　　 — Ich
16. *What do you believe, Karl?* Was glaubst _____ , Karl?　— du
17. *Today I play tennis.* Heute spiele _____ Tennis.　　— ich
18. *Who is she?* Wer ist _____?　　　　　　　　　　— sie
19. *She is not coming.* _____ kommt nicht.　　　　　 — Sie
20. *Karl and Udo, do you have time?* Karl und Udo habt _____
    Zeit?　　　　　　　　　　　　　　　　　　　 — ihr
21. *Renate and I like to dance.* Renate und _____ tanzen gern.　— ich
22. *Quiet, Lassie! You know Ms. Erika!* Ruhig, Lassie! _____
    kennst Fräulein Erika!　　　　　　　　　　　　　— Du

2. The definite articles **der, die, das**

23. The grammatical gender of German nouns may be either
    _____, _____, or _____.　　　　　　　　　　　— masculine, feminine,
    　　　　　　　　　　　　　　　　　　　　　　　　neuter

24. The grammatical gender of nouns designating people is
    usually the same as their biological sex. Two notable excep-
    tions, however, are _____ and _____.　　　　　　— **das Fräulein,
    　　　　　　　　　　　　　　　　　　　　　　　　das Mädchen**

25. All nouns with the diminutive endings **-chen** or **-lein** are
    _____.　　　　　　　　　　　　　　　　　　　— neuter

26. Many masculine German nouns can be made feminine by
    adding the ending _____.　　　　　　　　　　　— **-in**

Supply the appropriate definite article.

27.	*man*	_____ Mann	— der
28.	*woman*	_____ Frau	— die
29.	*concert*	_____ Konzert	— das
30.	*record*	_____ Platte	— die
31.	*student*	_____ Studentin	— die
32.	*daughter*	_____ Tochter	— die
33.	*son*	_____ Sohn	— der
34.	*girl*	_____ Mädchen	— das
35.	*vocabulary*	_____ Wortschatz	— der
36.	*little sister*	_____ Schwesterchen	— das

3. The gender of third-person pronouns

37. Pronouns must have the same gender as the _____ they
    stand for.　　　　　　　　　　　　　　　　　— noun

Complete with the appropriate pronoun.

38. Ist die Frau nett? Ja, _____ ist nett.　　　　　　— sie
39. Wie heißt die Studentin? _____ heißt Elke.　　　 — Sie

40. Ist das Konzert heute? Ja, _____ ist heute.   — es
41. Kommt der Bus? Ja, _____ kommt.   — er

4. The plural of nouns

42. In the plural, all German nouns have the same definite
    article: _____.   — die
43. All German nouns begin with a _____ letter.   — capital
44. German nouns form their plural by adding no ending at all,
    or by adding the endings _____, _____, _____, or _____.   — -e, -er, -en (or -n), -s
45. In addition, some nouns with the stem vowel **a, o,** or **u** may
    add an _____ in the plural.   — umlaut[1]
46. Nouns adding **-en** in the plural (always/never) umlaut.   — never

Supply the plural form according to the symbols indicated.

47. der Vater, ¨   _____ father   — die Väter
48. die Tochter, ¨   _____ daughter   — die Töchter
49. der Lehrer, —   _____ teacher   — die Lehrer
50. das Auto, —s   _____ car   — die Autos
51. der Tag, —e   _____ day   — die Tage
52. der Zug, ¨e   _____ train   — die Züge
53. das Kind, —er   _____ child   — die Kinder
54. das Haus, ¨er   _____ house   — die Häuser
55. die Platte, —n   _____ record   — die Platten
56. der Staat, —en   _____ state   — die Staaten

5. The plural of pronouns

57. The plural of the subject pronoun **er, sie, es** is _____.   — sie

Supply the appropriate pronoun.

58. Ist das Kind nett? Ja, _____ ist nett.   — es
59. Sind die Kinder nett? Ja, _____ sind nett.   — sie
60. Wie heißt die Platte? _____ heißt *Er und Sie.*   — Sie
61. Wie heißen die Platten? _____ heißen *Rock-Konzerte.*   — Sie
62. Was spielt der Herr dort? _____ spielt Tennis.   — Er
63. Was spielen die Herren hier? _____ spielen Tennis.   — Sie

Supply the German pronoun.

64. *She studies biology.* _____ studiert Biologie.   — Sie
65. *Are you coming?* Kommen _____?   — Sie
66. *What do they believe?* Was glauben _____?   — sie
67. *Who is she?* Wer ist _____?   — sie
68. *Who are you?* Wer sind _____?   — Sie

[1] **au** umlauts to **äu: Haus** > **Häuser**

69. *Is the record good? Yes, it is good.* Ist die Platte gut? Ja,
_____ ist gut.

— sie

6. sein and haben, present tense

Supply the correct form of sein.

70. Wir _____ Studenten.
71. _____ du Studentin?
72. Ja, ich _____ heute hier.
73. Ihr _____ sehr nett.
74. Er _____ leider nicht hier.
75. Herr Professor, _____ Sie heute hier?
76. Wer _____ sie (*they*)?
77. Wer _____ sie (*she*)?
78. Es _____ gut.

— sind
— Bist
— bin
— seid
— ist
— sind
— sind
— ist
— ist

Supply the correct form of haben.

79. Er _____ viel Zeit.
80. _____ wir keine Zeit?
81. _____ du die Platte?
82. Ihr _____ es.
83. Irene? Ja, sie _____ ein Auto.
84. _____ Karl und Irene heute Zeit?
85. Ja, wir _____ Arbeit.
86. Ich _____ die Platte nicht.
87. Es _____ Zeit.

— hat
— Haben
— Hast
— habt
— hat
— Haben
— haben
— habe
— hat

7. The infinitive

88. All German infinitives end in _____ or _____.
89. The stem of **tanzen** is _____; the stem of **studieren** is _____; the stem of **wandern** is _____

— -en, -n
— tanz-, studier-, wander-

8. The present tense of verbs

90. The **wir-**, **sie-**, and **Sie**-forms end in _____.
91. The **er/sie/es-** and **ihr**-forms end in _____.
92. The ending -st is added in the _____-form.
93. When the verb stem ends in -d or -t, a linking -e- is added in the _____, _____, and _____- forms to facilitate _____.

94. When the verb stem ends in a _____ sound, only _____ is added in the **du**-form (instead of -st).

— -en
— -t
— du

— du-, er-, ihr, pronunciation

— "hissing," -t

Supply all the possible pronouns that could be the subject for each item.

95. Spielen _____ heute Tennis?

— wir, sie, Sie

96. Glaubst _____ es?   — du
97. Kommt _____ heute?   — er, sie, ihr
98. Ja, _____ tanze gern.   — ich

Supply the appropriate verb ending.

99. Wie heiß___ du?   — -t
100. Ich hab___ es nicht.   — -e
101. Er spiel___ auch.   — -t
102. Glaub___ Sie es nicht?   — -en
103. Wo tanz___ du?   — -t
104. Ihr kenn___ es.   — -t
105. Du komm___ heute abend.   — -st
106. Glaub___ sie das?   — -t (*or* -en)
107. Wir studier___ auch.   — -en
108. Ihr find___ es dort.   — -et
109. Wer heirat___ nicht gern?   — -et
110. Du arbeit___ sehr gut.   — -est
111. Tanz___ sie gern?   — -t (*or* -en)
112. Lern___ du viel?   — -st

113. **Wir spielen** has three possible English equivalents:
     We _____, We _____, or We _____.   — *play, are playing, do play*

9. Verb-Subject word order in questions

114. In questions in German, the voice usually (rises/falls) toward the end.   — rises

115. The six most common question words in German are:
     *who? _____, what? _____, when? _____, where?
     _____, why? _____, how? _____.*   — **wer?, was?, wann?, wo?, warum?, wie?**

Change the statement into a question.

116. Er studiert. _____   — Studiert er?
117. Das Fräulein hat keine Zeit. _____   — Hat das Fräulein keine Zeit?
118. Es geht gut. _____   — Geht es gut?

10. The German alphabet

119. What seven letters rhyme with the letter **b**? ___, ___, ___, ___, ___, ___, ___.   — **c, d, e, g, p, t, w**

Erweitern Sie Ihren Wortschatz![1]

A. Englisch-Deutsch

1. girl _____

2. day _____

3. question _____

4. answer _____

5. record _____

6. night _____

7. student (female) _____

8. woman _____

9. to have _____

10. to be acquainted with _____

11. to believe _____

12. to come _____

13. to learn _____

14. to work _____

15. to understand _____

16. to live _____

17. to drink _____

18. to ask _____

19. but _____

20. what _____

21. much, many _____

22. correct, right _____

23. why _____

24. there is, there are _____

25. Good-bye! _____

[1] *Increase your vocabulary!* This exercise is designed to test how well you have mastered some of the basic vocabulary presented in each chapter. Write the equivalent of each word or expression in the blank provided. Where a German noun is asked for, give the appropriate definite article as well.

B. Deutsch-Englisch

1. die Zeit _____

2. das Beispiel _____

3. das Geld _____

4. die Wahrheit _____

5. der Wortschatz _____

6. die Bundesrepublik Deutschland _____

    _____

7. die Arbeit _____

8. die Tatsache _____

9. heißen _____

10. spielen _____

11. sein (ist) _____

12. lieben _____

13. studieren _____

14. denken _____

15. verwenden _____

16. zeigen _____

17. sagen _____

18. kaufen _____

19. heute _____

20. wer _____

21. sehr _____

22. wo _____

23. schlecht _____

24. die Freiheit _____

25. am Wochenende _____

Hör zu und antworte!   Antwortbogen

Übung **A**. *Circle* **Richtig** *or* **False**

1. R   F   2. R   F   F   4. R   F   5. R   F   6. R   F

Übung **B**. *Circle* **Logisch** *or* **Unlogisch**.

1. L   U   2. L   U   3. L   4. L   U   5. L   U   6. L   U

Übung **C**. *Circle A, B, or C.*

1. A   B   C   2. A   B   C   3.   B   C   4. A   B   C

5. A   B   C   6. A   B   C   7.   C   8. A   B   C

9. A   B   C   10. A   B   C   11. A   C

Übung **D**. *Circle the word you hear.*

Zimmer   Kalb   immer   schlecht   Vater

halb   aber   schlicht   gern   fern

Übung **E.** *Circle the correct English translation of the words you hear.*

1. work   time   6. comfortable   young

2. language   day   7. always   now

3. to love   to believe   8. to understand   to compare

4. to be   to save   9. to live   to love

5. lipstick   fact   10. to use   to say

Übung **F.** *Circle* **Logisch** *or* **Unlogisch**.

1. L   U   2. L   U   3. L   U   4. L   U   5. L   U

Kapitel 2

Selbst-Test

DIALOG

Translate the underlined expressions.

1. Von dort <u>gibt es</u> einen Bus.   — From there there is
2. <u>Das macht nichts</u>.   — That doesn't matter.
3. Hoffentlich <u>werden Sie nicht naß</u>.   — you will not get wet.
4. Er <u>weiß nichts</u>.   — knows nothing.

1. Verbs with a change in the stem vowel

5. In the present tense, some verbs change their stem vowel
   from **a** to _____, and from **e** to _____ or _____.   — **ä, i, ie**
6. These changes occur only in the _____- form and the
   _____/_____/_____-form.   — du, er/sie/es

Give the infinitive form of the verbs below.

7. du fährst _____   — fahren
8. sie gibt _____   — geben
9. er nimmt _____   — nehmen
10. sie sieht _____   — sehen
11. du ißt _____   — essen
12. sie spricht _____   — sprechen

Supply the correct verb form.

13. Wir essen zu viel. Du _____ zu viel.   — ißt
14. Ich gebe gern Auskunft. _____ er gern Auskunft?   — Gibt
15. Ihr sprecht gut Deutsch. Man _____ hier Deutsch.   — spricht
16. Wann fahren wir? Wann _____ der Bus?   — fährt
17. Ich nehme die Straßenbahn. _____ du auch die
    Straßenbahn?   — Nimmst

18. Sie spricht ziemlich gut Deutsch. _____ er auch gut? — Spricht
19. Ich trage keine Lederhosen. _____ du Lederhosen? — Trägst

2. The indefinite articles **ein** and **eine**

20. The indefinite articles that correspond to the definite
    articles are: **der,** _____; **die,** _____; **das,** _____. — ein, eine, ein

Supply the appropriate indefinite article.

21. Die Hausfrau arbeitet viel. _____ Hausfrau arbeitet viel. — Eine
22. Das Kaffeehaus ist gemütlich. _____ Kaffeehaus ist
    gemütlich. — Ein
23. Der Amerikaner ist anders. _____ Amerikaner ist anders. — Ein

3. kein: the negative form of **ein**

*Supply the correct form of **kein.***

24. Gibt es hier eine Bank? Nein, leider gibt es hier _____ Bank. — keine
25. Fährt heute ein Zug nach Düsseldorf? Nein, heute fährt
    _____ Zug dorthin. — kein
26. Haben Sie Fragen? Nein, ich habe _____ Fragen. — keine
27. Haben Sie Geld? Ich habe leider _____ Geld. — kein

Express in German.

28. I don't have any time. _____ — Ich habe keine Zeit.
29. I don't work. _____ — Ich arbeite nicht.
30. I don't have a radio. _____ — Ich habe kein Radio.

3a. The four cases: an overview (Optional: See Reference Grammar)

31. The four cases are: _____, _____, _____, and _____. — nominative, accusa-
                                                             tive, dative, genitive
32. The accusative is the case of the (direct/indirect) object. — direct
33. The genitive is the case of _____. — possession
34. Give the German equivalents: *who* _____, *whom* _____,
    to whom _____, *whose* _____. — **wer, wen,
                                          wem, wessen**

4. The accusative of definite and indefinite articles

35. The accusative forms are the same as the nominative, except
    for the _____ singular. — masculine
36. The nominative masculine singular is **der** and **ein**; the
    accusative masculine singular is _____ and _____. — **den, einen**

Supply the accusative form of the cue article.

37. (der Amerikaner) Ich kenne _____ Amerikaner.   — den
38. (die Amerikanerin) Er kennt _____ Amerikanerin.   — die
39. (das Mädchen) Ich frage _____ Mädchen.   — das
40. (die zwei Mädchen) Wir fragen _____ zwei Mädchen.   — die
41. (das Geld) Ich habe _____ Geld.   — das
42. (die Antwort) Wir wissen _____ Antwort.   — die
43. (der Zug) Nimmst du _____ Zug?   — den
44. (ein Bier) Gut, ich trinke _____ Bier.   — ein
45. (ein Walzer) Ich tanze gern _____ Walzer.   — einen
46. (eine Lederhose) Ja, sie trägt _____ Lederhose.   — eine
47. (keine Auskunft) Er gibt _____ Auskunft.   — keine
48. (kein Bus) Ich sehe _____ Bus.   — keinen
49. (keine Zeit) Sie hat _____ Zeit.   — keine
50. (keine Kinder) Sie haben _____ Kinder.   — keine

5. The accusative of personal pronouns

51. For each nominative form of the personal pronoun, give the
accusative form:

ich, _____; **du,** _____; **er,** _____; **sie,** _____;   — mich, dich, ihn, sie,
es, _____; **wir,** _____; **ihr,** _____; **sie,** _____;   es, uns, euch, sie,
Sie, _____.   Sie

Supply the accusative form of the personal pronoun.

52. (*Are you asking me?*) Fragen Sie _____?   — mich
53. (*Do you know her?*) Kennen Sie _____?   — sie
54. (*Are you marrying him?*) Heiratest du _____?   — ihn
55. (*Do you understand us?*) Verstehen Sie _____?   — uns
56. (*Do you love them?*) Liebst du _____?   — sie
57. (*Are you buying it?*) Kaufst du _____?   — es
58. (*Am I disturbing you?*) (familiar plural) Störe ich _____?   — euch
59. (*Am I disturbing you?*) (formal singular) Störe ich _____?   —Sie

Restate each sentence, switching the subject and the direct object.

60. Du verstehst mich. _____   — Ich verstehe dich.
61. Er fragt sie. _____   — Sie fragt ihn.
62. Wir sehen euch. _____   — Ihr seht uns.
63. Sie kennen uns. _____   — Wir kennen Sie *or* sie.
64. Ich liebe dich. _____   — Du liebst mich.
65. Heiratet sie ihn? _____   — Heiratet er sie?
66. Ihr stört mich nicht. _____   — Ich störe euch nicht.

67. Kennen sie uns? _____   — Kennen wir sie?
68. Suchen Sie sie? _____   — Sucht sie Sie?

Supply the correct pronoun.

69. Der Wein ist gut. Ich trinke _____ gern.   — ihn
70. Das Bier ist gut. Ich kaufe _____ oft.   — es
71. Die Medizin ist schlecht. Ich nehme _____ nicht.   — sie
72. Die Traditionen sind alt und ich liebe _____.   — sie
73. Die Wahrheit? Ich weiß _____ nicht.   — sie
74. Der Vergleich ist falsch. Ich verstehe _____ nicht.   — ihn

6. The present tense of **wissen**

75. The stem vowel of **wissen** is different in the (singular/plural).   — singular
76. The **er-/sie-/es**-forms (do/do not) end in **-t**.   — do not
77. **Kennen** *to know* is used with concrete things and _____.   — persons
78. **Wissen** *to know* is used with abstract things and _____.   — ideas

Supply the correct form of **wissen** *or* **kennen,** *whichever is appropriate.*

79. Wir _____ nichts.   — wissen
80. Er _____ mich.   — kennt
81. Ich _____ es.   — weiß
82. Du _____ viel.   — weißt
83. Wir _____ Berlin gut.   — kennen
84. Irene _____ die Antwort.   — weiß
85. _____ Sie die Wahrheit?   — Wissen
86. _____ du den Wein?   — Kennst
87. Ihr _____ warum.   — wißt
88. _____ sie wo?   — Wissen

7. es gibt

89. The idiom **es gibt** *there is, there are* always takes the _____ case.   — accusative

Express in German.

90. There is no bus here. _____   — Es gibt hier keinen Bus.

91. But there is a train. _____   — Aber es gibt einen Zug.

92. Are there no female students here? _____   — Gibt es keine Studentinnen hier?

8. Verbal nouns

93. Verbal nouns in German have the same form as the _____   — infinitive

94. In English, verbal nouns end in (*-ing*).   — *-ing*

Complete the English equivalent.

95. Tanzen macht Spaß! _____ *is fun!*   — *Dancing*

96. Das Heiraten ist oft problematisch. _____ *is often*   — *Marrying*
    problematical.

97. Ist das Trinken schlecht? *Is* _____ *bad?*   — *drinking*

Erweitern Sie Ihren ~~rtschatz!~~

A. Englisch-Deutsch

1. car _____

2. minute _____

3. streetcar _____

4. mountain _____

5. sun _____

6. boy _____

7. city _____

8. customer *m* _____

9. store _____

10. flight _____

11. to _____

12. ~~k,~~ go _____

1 ~~become~~ _____

14. to write _____

15. to speak _____

16. to teach _____

17. nothing _____

18. inexpensive, cheap _____

19. large, big _____

20. important _____

21. where (to) _____

22. small, little _____

23. hopefully _____

24. isn't it? _____

25. free _____

B. Deutsch-Englisch

1. die Straße _____

2. der Regen _____

3. zu Fuß gehen _____

4. der Besuch _____

5. die Leute _____

6. die Post _____

7. die Reklame _____

8. das Meer _____

9. die Meinung _____

10. der Einkauf _____

11. fahren _____

12. werden _____

13. reisen _____

14. tragen _____

15. treffen _____

16. bedeuten _____

17. wieder _____

18. schon _____

19. schwer _____

20. also _____

21. vielleicht _____

22. fast _____

23. überall _____

24. noch nicht _____

25. recht haben _____

Hör zu . . .und antworte!   Antwortbogen

Übung **A**. *Circle* **Richtig** *or* **Falsch**.

1. R   F   2. R   F   3. R   F   4. R   F   5. R   F   6. R   F

Übung **B**. *Circle* **Logisch** *or* **Unlogisch**.

1. L   U   2. L   U   3. L   U   4. L   U   5. L   U   6. L   U

Übung **C**. *Circle* **Gleich** *or* **Ungleich**.

1. G   U   2. G   U   3. G   U   4. G   U   5. G   U   6. G   U

Übung **D**. *Circle* **Ja** *or* **Nein**.

1. Ja   Nein   2. Ja   Nein   3. Ja   Nein   4. Ja   Nein   5. Ja   Nein

6. Ja   Nein   7. Ja   Nein   8. Ja   Nein   9. Ja   Nein   10. Ja   Nein

Übung **E**. *Circle* **Ja** *or* **Nein**.

1. Ja   Nein   2. Ja   Nein   3. Ja   Nein   4. Ja   Nein   6. Ja   Nein

6. Ja   Nein   7. Ja   Nein   8. Ja   Nein   9. Ja   Nein   10. Ja   Nein

Übung **F**. **Diktat**. *Supply punctuation marks.*

1. _____

2. _____

3. _____

A

B

C

D

E

F

Übung **G**. *Circle the number of the statement that applies to each picture.*

Picture A (Bild A)	1	2	3	4	5	6		Picture B (Bild B)	1	2	3	4	5	6
Picture C (Bild C)	1	2	3	4	5	6		Picture D (Bild D)	1	2	3	4	5	6
Picture E (Bild E)	1	2	3	4	5	6		Picture F (Bild F)	1	2	3	4	5	6

Kapitel 3

Selbst-Test

DIALOG

Translate the underlined expressions.

1. <u>Sehen Sie</u> nach rechts!   — Look
2. <u>Der Zug fährt</u> um zwanzig Uhr <u>ab</u>.   — The train departs
3. <u>Das ist nicht möglich</u>.   — That is not possible.
4. Glauben Sie, <u>daß ich</u> noch einen Platz <u>bekomme</u>?   — that I will get
5. Kein Problem, <u>wenn Sie</u> ein Taxi <u>nehmen</u>.   — if you take

1. The three word orders: an overview

6. The three word orders are: _____, _____, _____.   — Subject-Verb, Verb-Subject, Verb-Last

7. The three word orders are also called _____, _____, _____.   — normal, inverted, transposed or dependent

2. Subject-Verb word order

8. In a subject-verb sentence, the verb (precedes/follows) the subject.   — follows

3. Verb-Subject word order

9. Verb-Subject word order (is/is not) used in questions.   — is
10. The same word order is also used in formal _____.   — commands
11. In a question the voice _____, and in a command the voice _____.   — rises, falls
12. Verb-Subject word order is also used when the sentence begins with an element that is not the subject. This element is known as the _____ _____.   — front field
13. It may consist of a single word, a phrase, or a _____ _____.   — dependent clause

Begin the sentence with the underlined expression.

14. Jeans sind <u>heute</u> in Deutschland sehr populär. _____

— Heute sind Jeans in Deutschland sehr populär.

15. Man trägt viele Jeans <u>in Deutschland</u>. _____

— In Deutschland trägt man viele Jeans.

16. Man ist sehr populär, <u>wenn man Jeans trägt</u>. _____

— Wenn man Jeans trägt, ist man sehr populär.

Form a command using the cue words.

17. (den Fahrplan/Sie/lesen) _____

— Lesen Sie den Fahrplan!

18. (Sie/einen Augenblick/warten) _____

— Warten Sie einen Augenblick!

19. (nehmen/ein Taxi/Sie) _____

— Nehmen Sie ein Taxi!

4. Verb-Last word order

20. Verb-Last word order is used in _____ clauses.

— dependent

21. A dependent clause depends for its meaning on a _____ clause.

— main

22. Dependent clauses frequently begin with _____ conjunctions.

— subordinating

23. The three subordinating conjunctions you have learned so far are _____ *that,* _____ *because,* and _____ *whenever, if.*

— **daß, weil, wenn**

24. Main and dependent clauses are always separated by a _____.

— comma

Complete with the cue clause in V-L word order.

25. (ich bekomme einen Platz) Glauben Sie, daß _____

— ich noch einen Platz bekomme?

26. (Sie haben es eilig) Nehmen Sie ein Taxi, wenn _____

— Sie es eilig haben.

27. (es ist Sonntag) Heute fährt kein Schnellzug, weil _____

— es Sonntag ist.

Complete by rearranging the cue words in the appropriate word order.

28. (billig/wenn/die Charter-Flüge/sind), gibt es viele Touristen. _____   — Wenn die Charter-Flüge billig sind

29. Er fährt in die Alpen, (liebt/weil/die Berge/er). _____   — weil er die Berge liebt
30. Ich weiß, (die Deutschen/die Sonne/daß/suchen). _____   — daß die Deutschen die Sonne suchen

Supply **wenn** *or* **wann.**

31. _____ fährt der Zug nach Zürich?   — Wann
32. Fliegen Sie, _____ Sie es eilig haben!   — wenn
33. Ich fliege, _____ es nicht zu viel kostet.   — wenn
34. _____ ich Zeit habe, komme ich.   — Wenn

5. Separable-prefix verbs

35. A separable prefix (changes/does not change) the meaning of a root verb.   — changes

Give the German equivalent.

36. *to stand* _____, *to get up* _____   — stehen, aufstehen
37. *to hear* _____, *to stop* _____   — hören, aufhören
38. *to travel* _____, *to depart* _____   — fahren, abfahren
39. In separable-prefix verbs, the stress in speaking falls on the _____.   — prefix
40. In the infinitive, the prefix is part of the _____.   — verb
41. The separable prefix is separated from the root verb in a _____ clause in the present and past tenses, and in a _____ command.   — main, formal
42. When the separable prefix is separated, it comes at the _____ of the clause.   — end
43. In a dependent clause the verb stands at the end. Since the separable prefix also stands at the end of a dependent clause, the prefix and the root verb are (separated/joined).   — joined

Complete, placing the cue verb in the correct position.

44. (aufhaben) In Deutsch _____ wir immer zu viel _____.   — haben . . . auf
45. (aufstehen) Wann _____ du am Wochenende _____?   — stehst . . . auf
46. (mitkommen) _____ Sie doch _____!   — Kommen . . . mit
47. (ankommen) Er _____ heute abend um 20 Uhr _____.   — kommt . . . an
48. (aufhaben) Ich glaube nicht, daß wir zu viel _____.   — aufhaben
49. (mitkommen) Wir haben es gern, wenn Sie _____.   — mitkommen
50. (ankommen) Du hast viel Zeit, weil der Zug pünktlich _____.   — ankommt

Restate the sentence, replacing the verb with the cue verb.

51. (anrufen) Wann telefonieren Sie Toni? Wann _____?
52. (anrufen) Wir warten, daß er Toni telefoniert. Wir warten, daß er _____.
53. (anrufen) Telefonieren Sie Toni heute abend! _____

— rufen Sie Toni an

— Toni anruft
— Rufen Sie Toni heute abend an!

Give the infinitive of the verb and its English equivalent.

54. Machen Sie Ihre Bücher auf! _____ _____
55. Machen Sie Ihre Bücher zu! _____ _____

— aufmachen *to open*
— zumachen *to close*

Give the sentences indicated, using the cue words.

56. FORMAL COMMAND (weiterlaufen/Sie) _____
57. QUESTION (wiederkommen/wann/du) _____

58. STATEMENT (abfahren/ich/um 8 Uhr) _____

59. DEPENDENT CLAUSE (ankommen/wenn/Sie) Rufen Sie an, _____.

— Laufen Sie weiter!
— Wann kommst du wieder?
— Ich fahre um 8 Uhr ab.

— wenn Sie ankommen

nach Haus(e) vs. zu Haus(e)

Supply zu or nach as appropriate.

60. Ich gehe jetzt _____ Haus.
61. Wohnst du _____ Haus?
62. Ich bin um 8 Uhr wieder _____ Haus.
63. Ich warte _____ Haus.
64. Er kommt heute _____ Haus.

— nach
— zu
— zu
— zu
— nach

Deceptive "look-alikes" or "false friends"

Many German words resemble English, but mean something very different. Below are some that you have learned thus far. Give the correct English equivalents.

65. German **also** corresponds to English _____.
66. German **bekommen** corresponds to English _____.
67. German **man** corresponds to English _____.
68. German **die Art** corresponds to English _____.
69. German **wer** corresponds to English _____.
70. German **fast** corresponds to English _____.

— *therefore, so*
— *to receive, get*
— *one, people, you*
— *kind, way, type*
— *who*
— *almost*

Erweitern Sie Ihren Wortschatz!

A. Englisch-Deutsch

1. railroad station _____

2. person _____

3. stamp _____

4. letter _____

5. friend _____

6. cake _____

7. news _____

8. ice cream; ice _____

9. bill _____

10. traffic _____

11. plane _____

12. to depart, leave _____

13. visit _____

14. to need; to use _____

15. to eat _____

16. to get up _____

17. to sit _____

18. to sell _____

19. tomorrow _____

20. when, if _____

21. quick(ly) _____

22. expensive _____

23. prohibited _____

24. something _____

25. at home _____

B. Deutsch-Englisch

1. der Platz _____

2. der Flughafen _____

3. der Sonntag _____

4. die Briefmarke _____

5. die Jugendherberge _____

6. der Wochentag _____

7. das Trinkgeld _____

8. die Autobahn _____

9. die Rechnung _____

10. die Zeitung _____

11. der Wetterbericht _____

12. stehen _____

13. anrufen _____

14. bekommen _____

15. mitnehmen _____

16. ankommen _____

17. vergessen _____

18. wohnen _____

19. bitte _____

20. wieviel _____

21. krank _____

22. bald _____

23. weil _____

24. täglich _____

25. bis _____

Hör zu . . .und antworte!   Antwortbogen

Übung **A**. *Circle* **Logisch** *or* **Unlogisch**.

1. L U	2. L U	3. L U	4. L U	5. L U
6. L U	7. L U	8. L U	9. L U	10. L U

Übung **B**. *Circle* **Richtig** *or* **Falsch**.

1. R F	2. R F	3. R F	4. R F	5. R F
6. R F	7. R F	8. R F	9. R F	10. R F

Übung **C**. **Diktat**.

1. _____

2. _____

3. _____

Übung **D**. *Circle* **Ja** *or* **Nein**.

1. Ja Nein	2. Ja Nein	3. Ja Nein	4. Ja Nein	5. Ja Nein
6. Ja Nein	7. Ja Nein	8. Ja Nein	9. Ja Nein	10. Ja Nein

A   B

Übung **E**. *Circle the number of the statement that applies to each picture.*

Picture A (**Bild A**) 1   2   Picture B (**Bild B**) 3   4

Übung **F**. *Write the answers to the questions on the paragraph you have heard.*

1. Warum geht John auf die Post? Er hat _____

2. Wer kommt mit auf die Post? _____

3. Wo ist John zu Haus? In _____

4. Was ist nicht so teuer, telefonieren oder telegrafieren? _____

5. Was weiß Susanne? In Deutschland _____

6. Warum weiß sie das? Sie ist _____

Übung **G**. *Circle A, B, or C, or a combination thereof.*

1. A B C   2. A B C   3. A B C   4. A B C   5. A B C   6. A B C

7. A B C   8. A B C   9. A B C   10. A B C   11. A B C   12. A B C

13. A B C   14. A B C   15. A B C   16. A B C   17. A B C   18. A B C

19. A B C   20. A B C   21. A B C   22. A B C   23. A B C   24. A B C

25. A B C   26. A B C

Kapitel 4

Selbst-Test

DIALOG

Translate the underlined expressions.

1. <u>Raten Sie</u>.   — Guess.
2. <u>Stehen Sie bitte auf!</u>   — Please get up.
3. Ich sehe <u>ihn</u>.   — him.
4. Das bedeutet <u>also</u>.   — therefore.

1. Prepositions governing the accusative

5. Five of the most common prepositions that govern the accusative are (give the English equivalent as well):

   _____ _____, _____ _____, _____ _____, _____ _____,
   _____ _____.
   — **durch** *through,* **für** *for,* **gegen** *against,* **ohne** *without,* **um** *around*

6. In everyday speech, **durch, für, über,** and **um** are contracted with the definite article when they occur with a (**der-/das-/die-**) noun.
   — **das-**

7. In idiomatic expressions, prepositions like **um** often have a meaning (different from/similar to) their usual one.
   — different from

8. **Um** may also mean _____ as in **um vier Uhr.**
   — at

Supply an appropriate preposition requiring the accusative.

9. Der Zug fährt _____ die Schweiz.   — durch
10. Ich habe nichts _____ dich.   — gegen
11. Die Post kommt immer _____ neun Uhr. — um
12. Wir sitzen _____ den Tisch.   — um
13. Kaufen Sie die Platte _____ ihn!   — für
14. Wir sprechen _____ das Wetter.   — über
15. Ich trinke Kaffee _____ Zucker.   — ohne

Complete the sentence as suggested by the cue, using the accusative.

16. (der Hotelportier) Das Trinkgeld ist für _____. — den Hotelportier
17. (der Bahnhof) Der Zug fährt durch _____. — den Bahnhof
18. (der Verkehr) Er fährt gegen _____. — den Verkehr
19. (das Haus) Man baut eine Straße um _____. — das Haus
20. (das Rauchen) Er kann ohne _____ nicht leben. — das Rauchen
21. (die Stadt) Die Straße geht durch _____. — die Stadt
22. (eine Straßenkarte) Wir reisen nie ohne _____. — eine Straßenkarte
23. (ein Amerikaner) Ich kaufe die Lederhose für _____. — einen Amerikaner
24. (du) Wir fahren ohne _____. — dich
25. (er) Ich habe nichts gegen _____. — ihn
26. (ich) Ich kaufe den Kaugummi für _____. — mich
27. (Sie) Der Brief ist für _____. — Sie
28. (sie *they*) Was machen Sie für _____? — sie
29. (sie *she*) Ich komme ohne _____. — sie
30. (wer) Für _____ machst du die Arbeit? — wen
31. (wir) Sind Sie für oder gegen _____? — uns

Complete as suggested by the cue noun. Contract the preposition with the definite article whenever possible.

32. (das Haus) Wir laufen um _____. — ums Haus
33. (den Bahnhof) Wir gehen um _____. — den Bahnhof
34. (das Kind) Zucker ist schlecht für _____. — fürs Kind
35. (der Hund) Butter ist nicht gut für _____. — den Hund
36. (der Berg) Ja, der Zug fährt durch _____. — den Berg
37. (die Straße) Fahren Sie durch _____! — die Straße
38. (das Geschäft) Gehen Sie durch _____! — durchs Geschäft

2. Separable-prefix verbs: review and expansion

Change the verb to the new meaning by adding the appropriate separable prefix.

39. fahren *to travel* *to depart* _____ — abfahren
40. fangen *to catch* *to begin* _____ — anfangen
41. hören *to hear* *to stop, to seize* _____ — aufhören
42. sehen *to see* *to look, appear* _____ — aussehen
43. laden *to load* *to invite* _____ — einladen
44. stehen *to stand* *to get up* _____ — aufstehen
45. nehmen *to take* *to gain weight* _____ — zunehmen

Restate, substituting the cue verb.

46. (wiedersehen) Wann siehst du ihn? Wann _____? — siehst du ihn wieder
47. (abfahren) Ja, wir fahren morgen. Ja, wir _____. — fahren morgen ab

48. (ankommen) Wann kommt der Zug? Wann _____? — kommt der Zug an
49. (anrufen) Rufen Sie uns! _____! — Rufen Sie uns an

3. Negation with **nicht**

50. **Kein** is the equivalent of English _____, _____, _____ — *not a, not any, no,* followed by a noun

51. **Kein** (not **nicht**) must be used when the direct object is a noun with no article at all or with (an indefinite/ a definite) article. — an indefinite

Negate the sentence.

52. Er hat ein Auto. Er hat _____. — kein Auto
53. Wir haben Zeit. Wir haben _____. — keine Zeit

Complete the negation.

54. Hat er Geld? Nein, er hat _____. — kein Geld
55. Hat er das Geld? Nein, er hat _____. — das Geld nicht
56. Although the position of **nicht** may vary, some guidelines are helpful. **Nicht** usually stands (in the middle/at the end) of a sentence when it negates the entire sentence. — at the end
57. When it does not go counter to the rules of word order, **nicht** (follows/precedes) that particular element which it negates. — precedes
58. **Nicht** precedes expressions of (place/time). — place
59. **Nicht** follows expressions of (place/time). — time

Negate the sentence.

60. Ich weiß es. Ich _____. — weiß es nicht
61. Er sagt, daß er es weiß. Er sagt, daß er _____. — es nicht weiß
62. Wissen Sie es? Wissen _____? — Sie es nicht
63. Ich fahre morgen mit. Ich fahre _____. — morgen nicht mit
64. Ich fahre morgen. Ich _____. — fahre morgen nicht
65. Ich fahre nach Zürich. Ich fahre _____. — nicht nach Zürich
66. Fahren Sie bitte schnell! Fahren Sie bitte _____! — nicht schnell
67. Das ist gut. Das _____. — ist nicht gut

4. The function of adverbs

68. An adjective communicates information about a _____. — noun
69. An adverb communicates information about another adverb, an _____, or a _____. — adjective, verb

70. The information communicated by an adverb usually
   pertains to _____, _____, or _____.   — time, manner, place
71. German adverbs (never/sometimes) have an ending.   — never
72. Adverbs usually appear in the following sequence: (time-
   place-manner/time-manner-place/place-manner-time).   — time-manner-place
73. Unlike English, in German the adverb is usually not placed
   between the subject and the _____.   — verb

Supply the German adjective or adverb.

74. *I play tennis very well.* Ich spiele Tennis sehr _____.   — gut
75. *The Wienerschnitzel is good.* Das Wienerschnitzel ist _____. — gut
76. *The train is punctual.* Der Zug ist _____.   — pünktlich
77. *The train departs punctually.* Der Zug fährt _____ ab.   — pünktlich

*Expand the sentence, inserting the cue adverbs in their best se-
quence.*

78. (leider/morgen) Sie fliegt nach Hause. Sie fliegt _____.   — morgen leider nach
                                                                 Hause
79. (jetzt/hier/gewöhnlich) Der Zug kommt pünktlich an.
   Der Zug kommt _____.   — jetzt gewöhnlich hier
                                                                 pünktlich an
80. (hier/immer/am Wochenende) Warum fahren die Autos
   so schnell? Warum fahren die Autos _____?   — am Wochenende
                                                                 immer so schnell hier

5. hin and her

81. **Hin** indicates direction (away from/toward) the speaker.   — away from
82. **Her** indicates direction (away from/toward) the speaker.   — toward
83. **Hin** and **her** may be combined not only with verbs, but
   also with the question word _____.   — **wo**

Supply **hin** *or* **her.**

84. Warum gehen Sie immer _____ und _____?   — hin, her
85. Ich bin zu Hause. Kommen Sie bitte _____.   — her
86. Der Taschenrechner ist zu Hause. Gehen Sie bitte _____ und — hin, her
   bringen Sie ihn _____!

Supply **wo, wohin,** *or* **woher.**

87. _____ arbeiten Sie?   — Wo
88. _____ fahren Sie?   — Wohin
89. _____ wohnen Sie?   — Wo
90. _____ gehen Sie?   — Wohin
91. _____ kommen Sie?   — Woher

92. _____ wissen Sie das?   — Woher
93. _____ fliegst du?   — Wohin
94. _____ spielen Sie?   — Wo

6. Compound nouns

95. German compound nouns take their gender from that of
    the (first/last) component.   — last
96. In some cases, a linking _____, _____, or _____ is in-   — -s-, -es-, -n-
    serted between the components.

Form a compound noun and give its English equivalent.

97. (der Nichtraucher *nonsmoker*/das Abteil *compartment*)

    _____   — das Nichtraucherabteil
                                                       nonsmoking
                                                       compartment

98. (der Tag *day*/die Temperatur *temperature*)

    _____   — die Tagestemperatur
                                                       today's temperature

99. (kauen *to chew*/der Gummi *gum*)

    _____   — der Kaugummi
                                                       chewing gum

100. (die Woche *week*/das Ende *end*)

    _____   — das Wochenende
                                                       weekend

101. (das Auto *car*/die Bahn *way*)

    _____   — die Autobahn *inter-*
                                                       state highway, turn-
                                                       pike

7. Cardinal numbers

102. Cardinal numbers are used in _____.   — counting
103. *Thirtieth* is (a cardinal/an ordinal) number. — an ordinal
104. In numerals, German uses a _____ where English uses a
    decimal point.   — comma

Which is correct?

105. Es ist (eins/ein) Uhr.   — ein
106. Eine englische Meile sind (1,600/1.600/1600) Kilometer.   — 1.600
107. In München leben (3,400,000/3.400.000) Menschen.   — 3.400.000

Erweitern Sie Ihren Wortschatz!

A. Englisch-Deutsch

1. scientist _____

2. physician _____

3. for example _____

4. degree (temperature) _____

5. to guess _____

6. gasoline _____

7. pocket calculator _____

8. fever _____

9. apple _____

10. air _____

11. to help _____

12. to guess _____

13. to swim _____

14. water _____

15. bottle _____

16. long _____

17. slow(ly) _____

18. high _____

19. simple _____

20. clear _____

21. against _____

22. approximately _____

23. for a long time _____

24. really _____

25. that will do, that's all right _____

_____

B. Deutsch-Englisch

1. der Wechsel _____

2. Stundenkilometer _____

3. das Wienerschnitzel _____

4. pro Stunde _____

5. das Maß _____

6. das Meterband _____

7. langsam _____

8. ausrechnen _____

9. der Wagen _____

10. die Geschwindigkeit _____

11. der Quadratkilometer _____

    _____

12. die Gewohnheit _____

13. der Kaugummi _____

14. das Benzin _____

15. stattfinden _____

16. der Durchmesser _____

17. zwischen _____

18. enthalten _____

19. aussehen _____

20. wiegen _____

21. heiß _____

22. von heute auf morgen _____

23. langsam, aber sicher _____

24. fremd _____

25. ganz _____

Hör zu . . . und antworte!   Antwortbogen

Übung **A.** *Circle A, B, or C.*

1. A   B   C   2. A   B   C   3. A   B   C   4. A   B   C

5. A   B   C   6. A   B   C

Übung **B.** *Circle* **Ja** *or* **Nein.**

1. Ja   Nein   2. Ja   Nein   3. Ja   Nein   4. Ja   Nein   5. Ja   Nein

6. Ja   Nein   7. Ja   Nein   8. Ja   Nein   9. Ja   Nein   10. Ja   Nein

Übung **C.** **Diktat.** *Supply punctuation marks.*

1. _____

2. _____

3. _____

Übung **D.** *Circle A, B or C.*

1. A   B   C   2. A   B   C   3. A   B   C   4. A   B   C

5. A   B   C   6. A   B   C   7. A   B   C   8. A   B   C

9. A   B   C   10. A   B   C

A   B   C

Übung **E.** *Write down the correct answer.*

Picture A (**Bild A**) _____

Picture B (**Bild B**) _____

Picture C (**Bild C**) _____

Kapitel 5

Selbst-Test

DIALOG

Translate the underlined expressions.

1. <u>Von wem</u> sprichst du?
2. <u>Was ist los mit ihnen?</u>

3. <u>Wer</u> allein ist, sucht Kontakt.
4. <u>Bei euch</u> gibt es keine Heiratsannoncen?

— About whom
— What's the matter
   with them?

— Whoever
— In your country (At
   your place)

1. The dative of the definite and indefinite articles

5. The dative is the case of the _____ object.
6. English signals the indirect object in one of two ways: by
   a _____ or by _____ _____.

7. German signals the indirect object by inflection, that is, by
   changing the _____ of the article.

— indirect

— preposition, word
   order

— form

The dative forms are:

8. **der** _____   **die** _____   **das** _____   **die** (*pl*) _____
9. **ein** _____   **eine** _____   **ein** _____   **keine** _____

— **dem, der, dem, den**
— **einem, einer, einem,
   keinen**

10. The consonant _____ is the characteristic ending for both
   the masculine and _____.
11. In the dative, **der** becomes the _____ form.
12. In the dative plural, German nouns end in _____ or
   _____.
13. An exception is nouns that form their plural by adding
   _____.

— **m**, neuter

— feminine

— **-en, -n**

— **-s**

14. Most nouns (change/do not change) their form in the dative singular.

— do not change

15. An exception is masculine nouns that form their plural in _____.

— -en

Restate, substituting the cue noun.

16. (der Passant) Er zeigt der Frau die Haltestelle. Er zeigt _____ die Haltestelle.

— dem Passanten

17. (der Student) Er gibt der Studentin eine Zeitung. Er gibt _____ eine Zeitung.

— dem Studenten

18. (der Herr) Sie gibt dem Fräulein die Auskunft. Sie gibt _____ die Auskunft.

— dem Herrn

19. (die Kinder) Wir schreiben der Zeitung einen Brief. Wir schreiben _____ einen Brief.

— den Kindern

20. (das Kind) Er gibt dem Jungen das Eis. Er gibt _____ das Eis.

— dem Kind

21. (die Verkäuferin) Er gibt dem Verkäufer das Geld. Er gibt _____ das Geld.

— der Verkäuferin

Change the noun into the plural, or vice versa.

22. Ich verkaufe es dem Mädchen. Ich verkaufe es _____.

— den Mädchen

23. Er zeigt es den Lehrern. Er zeigt es _____.

— dem Lehrer

24. Es gehört den Studenten. Es gehört _____.

— dem Studenten

25. Wir schreiben den Lehrerinnen. Wir schreiben _____.

— der Lehrerin

Replace the definite article by the appropriate form of **ein** *or* **kein**.

26. Ich schreibe der Zeitung. Ich schreibe _____ Zeitung.

— einer (*or* keiner)

27. Wir helfen dem Amerikaner. Wir helfen _____ Amerikaner.

— einem (*or* keinem)

28. Wir zeigen das Foto den Amerikanerinnen. Wir zeigen das Foto _____ Amerikanerinnen.

— keinen

29. Es gehört den Touristen. Es gehört _____ Touristen.

— keinen

30. Er antwortet dem Mädchen. Er antwortet _____ Mädchen.

— einem (*or* keinem)

31. Es gehört dem Studenten. Es gehört _____ Studenten.

— einem (*or* keinem)

32. Ich zeige es der Polizistin. Ich zeige es _____ Polizistin.

— einer (*or* keiner)

Give the dative forms.

	NOMINATIVE	DATIVE SINGULAR	DATIVE PLURAL	
33.	der Mann	_____	_____	— dem Mann, den Männern
34.	die Frau	_____	_____	— der Frau, den Frauen
35.	das Kind	_____	_____	— dem Kind, den Kindern

36. der Student _____ _____ — dem Studenten,
    den Studenten

2. The dative of personal pronouns

Give the dative forms.

37. NOMINATIVE ich   du   er   sie   es
    DATIVE   ____ ____ ____ ____ ____   — mir, dir, ihm, ihr, ihm

38. NOMINATIVE wir   ihr   sie   Sie
    DATIVE   ____ ____ ____ ____   — uns, euch, ihnen,
                                                            Ihnen

Supply the German equivalent of the cue pronoun.

39. (*to me*) Er zeigt _____ die Annonce.   — mir
40. (*to her*) Er gibt _____ die Zeitung.   — ihr
41. (*to you* familiar singular) Sie schreibt _____.   — dir
42. (*to us*) Es gehört _____.   — uns
43. (*them*) Antworten Sie _____!   — ihnen
44. (*to you*) Gehört das _____, Fräulein Dietrich?   — Ihnen
45. (*you*) Wie geht es _____, Kinder?   — euch

Complete, replacing the article and noun with the appropriate pronoun.

46. Ich gebe es einem Freund. Ich gebe es _____.   — ihm
47. Wir bringen es einer Freundin. Wir bringen es _____. — ihr
48. Ich verkaufe es einem Kind. Ich verkaufe es _____.   — ihm
49. Er gibt es den Eltern. Er gibt es _____.   — ihnen

3. Prepositions governing the dative

50. The prepositions that always require the dative are, in
    alphabetical order: _____, _____, _____, _____, _____ ,
    _____, _____, _____.   — aus, außer, bei, mit,
                                                            nach, seit, von, zu

51. When **seit** refers to time, it corresponds to English _____.   — *for*
52. **Nach** corresponds to English *after, toward,* or _____.   — *according to*
53. Two of the following cannot be contracted. Which ones?
    bei dem, bei der, von dem, von der, zu dem, zu der   — **bei der, von der**

Complete with a dative preposition that makes sense.

54. Er antwortet immer _____ einem Klischee.   — mit
55. Sie wohnt _____ einem Jahr in Bern.   — seit
56. Wir besuchen euch _____ dem Wochenende.   — nach
57. Er fliegt morgen _____ Amerika.   — nach
58. Ich gehe jetzt _____ Bahnhof.   — zum
59. Ja, das Baby trinkt _____ der Flasche!   — aus

60. Wir sind _____ gestern wieder zu Haus.   — seit
61. Er wohnt immer noch _____ den Eltern.   — bei

Respond by completing with the dative of the cue noun.

62. (der Campingplatz)   Woher kommst du jetzt?

    Ich komme jetzt _____.   — vom Campingplatz

63. (eine Woche)   Seit wann wohnen Sie hier?

    Ich wohne _____ hier.   — seit einer Woche
64. (die Eltern)   Bei wem wohnst du jetzt?

    Ich wohne jetzt _____.   — bei den Eltern
65. (ein Freund)   Mit wem tanzt sie?

    Sie tanzt _____.   — mit einem Freund
66. (eine Freundin)   Mit wem spielst du heute?

    Ich spiele heute _____.   — mit einer Freundin

4. Verbs governing the dative

67. Some common verbs that govern the dative are: *to answer*
    _____, *to thank* _____, *to please* _____, *to belong* _____,   — **antworten, danken,**
    to believe _____, *to help* _____.   **gefallen, gehören,**
    glauben, helfen

Supply the dative of the cue expression.

68. (er) Ich glaube _____ nicht.   — ihm

69. (das Mädchen) Es gefällt _____.   — dem Mädchen

70. (der Professor) Ich antworte _____.   — dem Professor

71. (der Kunde) Sie dankt _____.   — dem Kunden

72. (die Leute) Wir helfen _____.   — den Leuten

73. (die Kundin) Es gehört _____.   — der Kundin

74. (sie *her*) Ich glaube _____.   — ihr

75. (ich) Das Foto gefällt _____.   — mir

5. Two-way prepositions

76. The nine prepositions that govern either the accusative or the dative are, in alphabetical order: _____, _____, _____, _____, _____, _____, _____, _____, _____.

— an, auf, hinter, in, neben, über, unter, vor, zwischen

77. The two-way prepositions all indicate (time/location).   — location

78. These prepositions take the accusative when they answer the question _____ (English _____).   — Wohin?, *Where to?*

79. They take the dative when they answer the question _____ (English _____).   — Wo?, *Where?*

80. When they express motion from one place to another, they take the (dative/accusative).   — accusative

81. When they express position in a place, they take the (dative, accusative).   — dative

82. When the verb indicates motion within a place, they take the (accusative/dative).   — dative

Complete the answer, putting the cue noun into the proper case.

(das Geschäft)

83. Wo ist Karl? (In) _____.   — Im [In dem] Geschäft

84. Wohin geht Karl? (In) _____.   — Ins [In das] Geschäft

85. Wo arbeitet Karl? (In) _____.   — Im [in dem] Geschäft

(die Bank)

86. Wo liegt das Geld? Auf _____.   — der Bank

87. Wohin bringst du das Geld? Auf _____.   — die Bank

(die Tafel)

88. Wo steht die Hausaufgabe? An _____.   — der Tafel

89. Wohin schreibt die Lehrerin die Hausaufgabe? An_____

_____.   — die Tafel

Complete with the appropriate verb of motion or rest.

90. (sitzen/gehen) Wir _____ ins Kaffeehaus.   — gehen
91. (fährt/steht) Das Auto _____ vor dem Haus.   — steht
92. (schreibe/wohne) Ich _____ an die Adresse.   — schreibe
93. (Warten/Gehen) _____ Sie hinter das Haus!   — Gehen

Complete.

94. Der Hund liegt hinter der Tür.

    Der Hund läuft hinter _____.   — die Tür
95. Er geht ins Geschäft.

    Er ist _____.   — im Geschäft
96. Sie sitzen an dem Tisch.

    Sie gehen an _____.   — den Tisch

What is the correct translation?

97. *The dog lies under the bed.* Der Hund liegt unter (den/dem) Tisch.   — dem
98. *The dog runs under the table.* Der Hund läuft unter (den/dem) Tisch.   — den
99. *The picture hangs between the radio and the door.* Das Bild hängt zwischen (das/dem) Radio und (die/der) Tür.   — dem, der
100. *He hangs the picture between the radio and the door.* Er hängt das Bild zwischen (das/dem) Radio und (die/der) Tür.   — das, die

6. Familiar commands

101. The formal command consists of the _____ plus the pronoun _____ or _____.   — infinitive, **Sie, wir**
102. In familiar commands the _____ is dropped.   — pronoun
103. The **du**-command consists of the (stem/infinitive) plus the ending _____.   — stem, **-e**
104. The ending is usually omitted, except in verbs that insert a linking _____.   — **-e-**
105. The **ihr**-command is the same as the **ihr**-form of the present tense, minus the _____.   — pronoun
106. Some verbs change the vowel in the **du**- command from **e** to _____ or _____.   — -i, -ie

Give the corresponding familiar command.

107. Kommen Sie! _____ — Komm!

108. Kommen Sie mit mir! _____ — Komm mit mir!

109. Antworten Sie auf deutsch! _____ — Antworte auf
    deutsch!

110. Seien Sie geduldig! _____ — Sei geduldig!

111. Sprechen Sie Deutsch! _____ — Sprich Deutsch!

112. Warten Sie hier! _____ — Warte hier!

113. Gehen Sie weiter! _____ — Geh weiter!

Change from the singular to the plural, and vice versa.

114. Schreibt einen Brief! _____ einen Brief!   — Schreib

115. Wartet auf mich! _____ auf mich!   — Warte

116. Hilf mir! _____ mir!   — Helft

117. Eßt nicht so viel! _____ nicht so viel!   — Iß

118. Steh auf! _____   — Steht auf!

119. Vergeßt mich nicht! _____ mich nicht!   — Vergiß

120. Fang an! _____   — Fangt an!

121. Gebt dem Hund Wasser! _____ dem Hund Wasser!   — Gib

Translate.

122. *Let's speak German!* _____ — Sprechen wir
    Deutsch!

123. *Let's stay here!* _____ hier!   — Bleiben wir

124. *Fritz, be nice!* Fritz, _____ !   — sei nett!

125. *Ulrike, don't eat so much!* Ulrike, _____!   — iß nicht so viel!

7. Word order of direct and indirect objects

126. The indirect object usually precedes the direct object, unless
    the direct object is a _____. All pronouns _____ nouns.   — pronoun precede

Complete, changing the underlined words into pronouns.

127. Er schreibt der Zeitung einen Brief.

    Er schreibt _____.   — ihr einen Brief

128. Er schreibt der Zeitung einen Brief.

Er schreibt _____. — ihn der Zeitung

129. Er schreibt der Zeitung einen Brief.

Er schreibt _____. — ihn ihr

130. Wer zahlt dem Arzt die Rechnung?

Wer zahlt _____? — sie dem Arzt

131. Wer zahlt dem Arzt die Rechnung?

Wer zahlt _____? — ihm die Rechnung

132. Wer zahlt dem Arzt die Rechnung?

Wer zahlt _____? — sie ihm

bekommen vs. werden

133. *I get money.* Ich _____ Geld. — bekomme
134. *He receives nothing.* Er _____ nichts. — bekommt
135. *He is getting old.* Er _____ alt. — wird
136. *Are you getting sick?* _____ Sie krank? — Werden
137. *Who gets the bill?* Wer _____ die Rechnung? — bekommt

Complete with the correct form of werden.

138. *I get tired quickly.* Ich _____ schnell müde. — werde

139. *You are getting fat, Oskar!* Du _____ dick,

Oskar! — wirst

140. *He is going to be (becoming) a teacher.* Er _____

Lehrer. — wird

141. *Lea is getting to be prettier and prettier.* Lea _____

immer hübscher. — wird

142. *It is getting colder.* Es _____ kälter. — wird

143. *How does one become rich?* Wie _____ man

reich? — wird

144. *We are getting poorer and poorer.* Wir _____

immer ärmer.   — werden

145. *Why are you getting angry?* Warum _____ ihr

böse?   — werdet

146. *The rich are getting richer and richer.* Die Reichen

_____ immer reicher.   — werden

147. *Sir, don't be (become) fresh with me!* Mein Herr,

_____ Sie nicht frech mit mir!   — werden

Auflagenstärkste Zeitungen in der Bundesrepublik Deutschland

Name der Zeitung	Verlagsort	1. Halbjahr 1981 verkaufte Auflage
Bild-Zeitung	Hamburg	4,7 Millionen
Bild am Sonntag (Sonntagsausgabe von „Bild")	Hamburg	2,5 Millionen
Westdeutsche Allgemeine Zeitung	Essen	1,2 Millionen
Rheinische Post	Düsseldorf	396 000
Münchener Merkur	München	344 000
Welt am Sonntag (Sonntagsausgabe der „Welt")	Hamburg	326 000
Frankfurter Allgemeine Zeitung	Frankfurt	324 000
Süddeutsche Zeitung	München	319 000
BZ	Berlin (West)	311 000
Hamburger Abendblatt	Hamburg	277 000
Die Welt	Hamburg	216 000
Die Zeit	Hamburg	386 000
Deutsches Allgemeines Sonntagsblatt	Hamburg	130 000

Auflagenstärkste Zeitschriften in der Bundesrepublik Deutschland (Publikumszeitschriften)

Name der Publikation	Verlagsort	1. Halbjahr 1981 verkaufte Auflage (in Millionen Exemplaren)
Neue Post	Hamburg	1,9
Stern	Hamburg	1,7
Tina	Hamburg	1,7
Burda-Moden (Monatsmagazin)	Offenburg	1,5
Bunte Illustrierte	Offenburg	1,4
Brigitte	Hamburg	1,3
Das Neue Blatt	Hamburg	1,3
Bravo	München	1,3
Neue Revue	Hamburg	1,2
Frau im Spiegel	Lübeck	1,1
Für Sie	Hamburg	1,0
Quick	München	1,0
Der Spiegel	Hamburg	0,9

Source: Inter Nationes

Erweitern Sie Ihren Wortschatz!

A. Englisch-Deutsch

1. table _____
2. mother _____
3. land, country _____
4. fun _____
5. wish _____
6. office _____
7. profession, job _____
8. leisure time _____
9. marriage ad _____
10. to remain _____
11. to seem _____
12. to marry _____
13. to earn _____

14. to understand _____
15. to do _____
16. to become a_ _ _ _ with, meet _____
   _____
1_. _ong _____
_. alone _____
19. single _____
20. friendly _____
21. slender _____
22. late _____
23. neither . . . nor _____
24. what's written in . . . ? _____
25. what's the matter? _____

B. Deutsch-Englisch

1. die Sitte _____
2. die Schönheit _____
3. die Freundschaft _____
4. die Freundin _____
5. die Lehrerin _____
6. München _____
7. der Nerv _____
8. klingen _____
9. warten auf _____
10. erfüllen _____
11. wir möchten _____
12. unglaublich _____
13. geschieden _____

14. anständig _____
15. evangelisch _____
16. manchmal _____
17. sympathisch _____
18. erst _____
19. treu _____
20. unfreundlich _____
21. genug _____
22. seriös _____
23. gar keine _____
24. unrecht tun _____
25. das paßt mir _____

Hör zu . . . und antworte!   Antwortbogen

Übung **A**.   *Circle A, B, or C.*

1. A   B   C   2. A   B   C   3. A   B   C   4. A   B   C

5. A   B   C   6. A   B   C

Übung **B**.   *Circle A, B, or C.*

1. A   B   C   2. A   B   C   3. A   B   C   4. A   B   C

5. A   B   C   6. A   B   C

Übung **C**.   *Circle **Ja** or **Nein**.*

1. Ja   Nein   2. Ja   Nein   3. Ja   Nein   4. Ja   Nein   5. Ja   Nein

6. Ja   Nein   7. Ja   Nein   8. Ja   Nein   9. Ja   Nein   10. Ja   Nein

Übung **D**.   *Circle A or B.*

1. A. Er gefällt ihr und sie gefällt ihm.   B. Du gefällst ihr und wir gefallen uns.

2. A. Er hat ein Kind.   B. Er möchte Kinder haben, aber er kann keine Kinder haben.

3. A. Sie ist verheiratet und eine werdende Mutti.   B. Sie ist nicht verheiratet und schwanger.

Übung **E**. *Circle the correct English word for the German cue.*

1. profession   friendship   2. teacher   leisure time   3. male friend   female friend

4. to remain   to earn   5. too bad   single   6. enough   late

7. to send   to marry   8. later   sometime   9. likable   that suits me

10. slender   single

Übung **F**. *Circle A or B, or both.*

1. A   B   2. A   B   3. A   B   4. A   B   5. A   B

6. A   B   7. A   B   8. A   B   9. A   B   10. A   B

Kapitel 6

Selbst-Test

DIALOG

Translate the underlined expressions.

1. <u>Möchtest du nicht?</u>
   — Wouldn't you like to?

2. Ich weiß nicht, <u>ob sie das akzeptieren können.</u>
   —whether they can accept that

3. <u>Sie will</u> bei mir <u>wohnen.</u>
   — She wants to live

4. <u>Ich möchte</u> unabhängig <u>bleiben.</u>
   — I would like to remain

1. Modal auxiliaries

5. The six modals grouped in pairs by their stem vowel are:
   o: _____, _____; ö _____, _____; ü _____, _____.
   — **sollen, wollen; können, mögen, dürfen, müssen**

The basic attitudes associated with the modals are:

6. dürfen _____ — permission
7. können _____ — ability
8. müssen _____ — duty
9. sollen _____ — imposed obligation
10. wollen _____ — intention

11. The modals are usually used in combination with an _____. — infinitive
12. In a main clause with a modal and an infinitive, the modal stands _____ of the clause. — at the end
13. In a dependent clause with a modal and an infinitive, the modal stands immediately (before/after) the infinitive. —after

14. The only modal that does not have a change in the stem vowel in the singular is _____.

— **sollen**

15. Any form of **möchte**, derived from **mögen**, always corresponds to English _____.

— *would like to*

16. German **will**, derived from **wollen**, never corresponds to English _____, but always to _____.

— *will, want*

17. The preposition **zu** is (sometimes/never) used to connect a modal and an infinitive.

— never

Supply the modal suggested by the cue.

18. (*may*) _____ ich rauchen?

— Darf

19. (*want to*) Ich _____ nicht rauchen.

— will

20. (*must*) _____ du immer so viel rauchen?

— Mußt

21. (*ought to*) Sie _____ nicht so viel rauchen.

— sollen

22. (*would like to*) Ich _____ nicht rauchen.

— möchte

23. (*wants to*) Er _____ jetzt nicht rauchen.

— will

24. (*can*) Sie _____ nicht mehr rauchen.

— kann

Restate, using the cue modal.

25. (können) Er spielt gut Tennis. Er _____.

— kann gut Tennis spielen

26. (wollen) Ich arbeite am Wochenende. Ich _____.

— will am Wochenende arbeiten

27. (sollen) Du denkst nicht nur an Geld. Du _____.

— sollst nicht nur an Geld denken

28. (müssen) Warum gehst du schon? Warum _____?

— mußt du schon gehen

29. (möchte) Ich tanze gern mit dir. Ich _____.

— möchte gern mit dir tanzen

30. (dürfen) Das tue ich nicht. Das _____.

— darf ich nicht tun

Complete, using the cue phrase.

31. Ich muß jetzt nach Haus(e) gehen.
Es tut mir leid, daß _____.

— ich jetzt nach Haus(e) gehen muß

32. Du willst bald heiraten.
Du mußt mehr Geld verdienen, wenn _____.

— du bald heiraten willst

33. Er kann jetzt noch nicht heiraten.
Er liest keine Heiratswünsche, weil _____.

— er jetzt noch nicht heiraten kann

34. Man darf hier rauchen.
Ich weiß nicht, ob _____.

— man hier rauchen darf

2. möchte

    35. The form **möchte** is derived from the infinitive _____.   — **mögen**

    36. Any form of **möchte** always means in English _____.   — *would like to*

Complete with the correct form of **möchte.**

    37. Wir _____ ein Zimmer.   — möchten

    38. _____ du mit mir zusammenwohnen?   — Möchtest

    39. Ich _____ gern heiraten.   — möchte

Supply the proper form of **wollen, möchte,** *or* **gern haben.**

    40. *He likes it.* Er _____ es _____.   — hat . . . gern

    41. *He would like to have it.* Er _____ es haben.   — möchte

    42. *What does he want?* Was _____ er?   — will

    43. *He would like to buy it.* Er _____ es kaufen.   — möchte

    44. *He does not want to do it.* Er _____ es nicht tun.   — will

3. More on subordinating conjunctions

Give the German equivalents.

    45. *when, as* _____   — **als**

    46. *until* _____   — **bis**

    47. *so that* _____   — **damit**

    48. *whether* _____   — **ob**

    49. *while, whereas* _____   — **während**

    50. *because* _____   — **weil** (or **da**)

    51. Subordinating conjunctions require (V-L/V-S) word order.   — V-L

Complete with an appropriate subordinating conjunction.

    52. Er will, _____ ich ihn heirate.   — daß

    53. Ich weiß nicht, _____ sie das wollen.   — ob

    54. Wir sparen, _____ wir heiraten können.   — damit

    55. Wir können nicht heiraten, _____ wir kein Geld haben.   — weil (*or* da)

    56. Wir warten, _____ wir mehr Geld haben.   — bis

Complete, arranging the cue words in the proper word order.

    57. (er/nicht/will/heiraten/weil)

    Er liest keine Heiratswünsche, _____

    _____   — weil er nicht heiraten will.

58. (hat/ob/sie/Zeit)

Fragen Sie sie, _____ — ob sie Zeit hat.

59. (eine Wohnung/haben/sie/Da)

_____,

können sie heiraten. — Da sie eine Wohnung haben,

Reverse the two clauses.

60. Ich habe nie Geld, obwohl ich immer spare.

_____ — Obwohl ich immer spare, habe ich nie Geld.

61. Sie dürfen nicht so viel essen, wenn Sie zu viel wiegen.

_____ — Wenn Sie zu viel wiegen, dürfen Sie nicht so viel essen.

62. Da es heute regnet, bleiben wir zu Hause.

_____ — Wir bleiben zu Hause, da es heute regnet.

Combine the two sentences with **sobald, während,** *or* **seit.**

63. Ich lese nicht mehr so viel. Ich habe einen Fernseher.

_____

_____ — Ich lese nicht mehr so viel, seit ich einen Fernseher habe.

64. Ich höre nicht mehr zu. Die Reklame kommt.

_____

_____ — Ich höre nicht mehr zu, sobald die Reklame kommt.

65. Ich kann nicht studieren. Das Radio spielt die ganze Zeit.

_____

_____

— Ich kann nicht studieren, während das Radio die ganze Zeit spielt.

4. Question words as subordinating conjunctions

66. When question words function as subordinating conjunctions, they introduce (direct/indirect) questions.

— indirect

67. When question words function as subordinating conjunctions, they cause (Verb-Last/Verb-Subject) word order.

— Verb-Last

Turn the direct question into an indirect question.

68. Wen kennt er hier? Er fragt, _____

_____.

— wen er hier kennt

69. Wo nennt man die Amerikaner „Amis"? Er will wissen,

_____?

— wo man die Amerikaner „Amis" nennt

70. Was kostet ein Flug nach Frankfurt? Können Sie mir sagen,

_____?

— was ein Flug nach Frankfurt kostet

Answer the question with an indirect question.

71. Wer ist das Mädchen dort?

Ich weiß nicht, _____.

— wer das Mädchen dort ist

72. Wie heißt der Junge dort?

Ich kann Ihnen nicht sagen, _____.

— wie der Junge dort heißt

73. Wem gehört das Auto hier?

Wer weiß, _____?

— wem das Auto hier gehört

Complete with the German equivalent of the cue word.

74. (*because*) Er raucht immer, _____ er nervös ist.   — weil (*or* da)
75. (*while*) Er raucht immer, _____ er arbeitet.   — während
76. (*since*) Er raucht so viel, _____ es eine Gewohnheit ist.   — da (*or* weil)
77. (*here, there*) Was machst du _____ ?   — da

5. Coordinating conjunctions

78. The five most common coordinating conjunctions are:
    _____ but, _____ because, for, _____ or, _____ but on
    the contrary, _____ and.   — **aber, denn, oder, sondern, und**

79. Coordinating conjunctions (change/do not change) word
    order.   — do not change

80. **Denn** and **weil** are interchangeable, but **weil** requires
    _____ word order.   — Verb-Last

81. The German two-part conjunction that corresponds to
    English *either . . . or* is _____ . . . _____ .   — **entweder . . . oder**

Complete with an appropriate coordinating or subordinating conjunction.

82. In Europa sendet man Telegramme nicht durch eine
    „Western Union", _____ durch die Post.   — sondern

83. In Österreich trinkt man viel Wein, _____ man trinkt
    auch viel Bier.   — aber

84. Das metrische System ist sehr einfach, _____ es ist
    dezimal.   — denn

85. Man benutzt das metrische System in den meisten Ländern,
    _____ es sehr praktisch ist.   — weil

86. Soll ich das Trinkgeld geben, _____ gibst du es?   — oder

87. _____ Sie schicken mir ein Foto, _____ ich schreibe nicht
    mehr.   — Entweder, oder

Complete with **denn** *or* **dann.**

88. Wir gehen jetzt essen, und _____ gehen wir ins Kino.   — dann
89. Wir gehen jetzt essen, _____ es ist ein Uhr.   — denn
90. Wenn Sie am Sonntag telefonieren, _____ ist es nicht so
    teuer.   — dann

6. The genitive case

91. The genitive communicates not only possession, but also a
    relationship between two nouns in which something is a
    _____ of something else.   — part

92. The characteristic genitive ending for masculine and neuter nouns in the singular is _____.   — -(e)s
93. Feminine nouns (do/do not) have an ending.   — do not
94. The characteristic genitive ending for the definite and indefinite articles in the masculine and neuter singular is _____.   — -es
95. In the feminine, the characteristic ending for the definite and indefinite articles is _____.   — -er
96. Plural nouns (never/sometimes) add an ending.   — never
97. **Studenten**-type nouns refer to masculine living beings. They form their plural in _____.   — -en
98. They add an _____ in the genitive singular, as they do in all cases except the _____ singular.   — -en, nominative
99. All proper names add _____ in the genitive.   — -s
100. Unlike English nouns, German nouns do not use an _____, unless the noun ends in an **s**-sound.   — apostrophe
101. In English, the possessor usually (precedes/follows) the common noun possessed.   — precedes
102. In German, the possessor usually (precedes/follows) the common noun possessed.   — follows
103. With proper nouns, German and English (follow/do not) the same word order.   — follow

Complete with the genitive form of the cue article.

104. (das) Die Tür _____ Zimmers ist offen.   — des
105. (die) Die Tür _____ Wohnung ist offen.   — der
106. (die) Die Türen _____ zwei Zimmer sind offen.   — der
107. (der) Die Tür _____ Ladens ist offen.   — des
108. (ein) Was ist der Preis _____ Zeltes?   — eines
109. (ein) Was ist der Preis _____ Wohnung?   — einer
110. (ein) Was ist der Preis _____ Hauses?   — eines

Complete with the genitive form of the cue noun.

111. (das Haus) Die Garage _____ ist zu klein.   — des Hauses
112. (die Häuser) Die Garagen _____ sind zu klein.   — der Häuser
113. (der Student) Wissen Sie den Namen _____?   — des Studenten
114. (die Studentin) Was ist die Adresse _____?   — der Studentin
115. (die Studenten) Die Antworten _____ sind gut.   — der Studenten
116. (der Arzt) Das Auto _____ ist kaputt.   — des Arztes
117. (die Lehrerin) Hier ist die Adresse _____.   — der Lehrerin
118. (Karl) Wie heißt _____ Freundin?   — Karls
119. (Ingrid) Wer ist _____ Freund?   — Ingrids
120. (Sokrates) _____ Philosophie lebt noch heute.   — Sokrates'
121. (die Fotos) Haben Sie die Negative _____?   — der Fotos

7. Telling time

122. The German preposition that corresponds to English *at* in telling time is _____.

— **um**

123. When expressing half hours, Germans usually count (after/ toward) the hour.

— toward

Express in German.

124. One o'clock _____

— Ein Uhr

125. A quarter after one _____

— Viertel nach eins

126. Twelve thirty _____

— Halb eins

127. Twenty to four _____

— Zwanzig vor vier

Complete, using the 24-hour system.

128. (*5 AM*) Es ist jetzt _____.

— fünf Uhr

129. (*7:30 AM*) Es ist jetzt _____.

— sieben Uhr dreißig

130. (*11: 34 AM*) Es ist jetzt _____.

— elf Uhr vierund- dreißig

131. (*5 PM*) Es ist jetzt _____.

— siebzehn Uhr

132. (*8:45 PM*) Es ist jetzt _____.

— zwanzig Uhr fünf- undvierzig

133. (*10:03 PM*) Es ist jetzt _____.

— zweiundzwanzig Uhr drei

134. (*midnight*) Es ist jetzt _____.

— null Uhr

Express in German.

135. *What time is it?* _____

— Wieviel Uhr ist es?

136. *It is one o'clock.* _____

— Es ist ein Uhr.

137. *It was a year ago.* _____

— Es war vor einem Jahr.

138. *It is five to one.* _____

— Es ist fünf vor eins.

139. *I am coming at half past six o'clock.* _____

— Ich komme um halb sieben.

Erweitern Sie Ihren Wortschatz!

A. Englisch-Deutsch

1. dormitory _____

2. apartment _____

3. room _____

4. advantage _____

5. examination _____

6. job, position _____

7. father _____

8. patient _____

9. idea _____

10. fiancée _____

11. school _____

12. end _____

13. to be together _____

14. to be able to, can _____

15. to lie, to be in bed _____

16. to room together _____

17. unmarried _____

18. independent _____

19. before _____

20. open(ly) _____

21. happy _____

22. it's a matter of, it concerns _____

23. we are not of the opinion _____

24. to take an exam _____

25. to be afraid of _____

B. Deutsch-Englisch

1. das Mittelalter _____

2. die Entscheidung _____

3. die Eltern _____

4. der Ruf _____

5. die Aufregung _____

6. der Herzanfall _____

7. die Zukunft _____

8. die Nummer _____

9. wollen _____

10. müssen _____

11. dürfen _____

12. durchfallen _____

13. schockieren _____

14. ob _____

15. beide _____

16. erlaubt _____

17. fertig _____

18. alles _____

19. solange _____

20. wahrscheinlich _____

21. stolz _____

22. nächst- _____

23. Toll! _____

24. alles Liebe _____

25. Sehr geehrter Herr! _____

Hör zu . . . und antworte!   Antwort bogen

Übung **A**. *Circle* **Richtig** *or* **Falsch**.

1. R F   2. R F   3. R F   4. R F   5. R F   6. R F

Übung **B**. *Circle* **Ja** *or* **Nein**.

1. Ja   Nein   2. Ja   Nein   3. Ja   Nein   4. Ja   Nein   5. Ja   Nein

6. Ja   Nein   7. Ja   Nein   8. Ja   Nein   9. Ja   Nein   10. Ja   Nein

Übung **C**. *Circle A, B or C. At times more than one response is possible.*

1. A   B   C   2. A   B   C   3. A   B   C   4. A   B   C

5. A   B   C   6. A   B   C   7. A   B   C   8. A   B   C

9. A   B   C   10. A   B   C   11. A   B   C   12. A   B   C

13. A   B   C   14. A   B   C   15. A   B   C   16. A   B   C

Übung **D**. *Circle* **Ja** *or* **Nein**.

1. Ja   Nein   2. Ja   Nein   3. Ja   Nein   4. Ja   Nein   5. Ja   Nein

6. Ja   Nein   7. Ja   Nein   8. Ja   Nein   9. Ja   Nein   10. Ja   Nein

Kapitel 7

Selbst-Test

DIALOG

Translate the underlined expressions.

1. Wie lange seid ihr verheiratet?

    — have you been married

2. Da hast du wohl an mich gedacht.
3. Wir haben für ein neues Auto gespart.
4. Was nicht ist, kann noch werden.

    — you have thought
    — We have saved
    — can still happen

1. Present perfect

5. The five major tenses are: _____, _____, _____, _____, _____.

    — present, past, present perfect, past perfect, future

6. In general, German-speaking people use the (past/present perfect) when talking about past events.

    — present perfect

7. The present perfect is also known as the _____ _____.

    — conversational past

8. The present perfect is called a compound tense because it is formed with an auxiliary and a _____ _____.

    — past participle

9. Most German verbs form their present perfect with the auxiliary _____.

    — **haben**

2. Position of the past participle

10. In a main clause, the past participle stands at (the beginning/the end) of the clause.

    — the end

11. In a dependent clause, the (past participle/conjugated verb) stands at the end.

    — conjugated verb

*Form a sentence or question, putting all the cue expressions into the
correct word order.*

12. (gehört/ich/habe/heute morgen/den Wetterbericht)

_____

_____ .

— Ich habe heute morgen den Wetterbericht gehört

13. (Sie/heute morgen/den Wetterbericht/haben/gehört)

_____

_____ ?

— Haben Sie heute morgen den Wetterbericht gehört

14. (gehört/den Wetterbericht/heute morgen/hat/er)

Er sagt, daß _____

_____ .

— er heute morgen den Wetterbericht gehört hat

3. haben and sein as auxiliary in the present perfect

15. In order to be conjugated with **sein** instead of **haben**, a German verb must fulfill (two/three) conditions.

— two

16. The first condition is that the verb must denote either a change of _____ or _____.

— place, condition

17. The second condition is that the verb must be (transitive/intransitive).

— intransitive

18. An intransitive verb is one that cannot take (a direct object/an indirect object).

— a direct object

19. *Does sentence* a) *or sentence* b) *contain a direct object?*
    a) Er ist mit einem Porsche gefahren.
    b) Er hat einen Porsche gefahren.

— b)

Do the following verbs denote a change of condition, a change of place, or neither?

20. **laufen** to run _____

— change of place

21. **hören** to hear _____

— neither

22. **werden** to become _____

— change of condition

23. **durchfallen** to fail _____

— change of condition

24. **wohnen** to inhabit _____

— neither

25. **sterben** to die _____

— change of condition

Five other verbs also use **sein** *as the auxiliary:*

26. *to remain* _____   — **bleiben**
27. *to happen* _____ or _____   — **geschehen, passieren**
28. *to succeed* _____   — **gelingen**
29. *to be* _____   — **sein**

Supply the appropriate form of **haben** *or* **sein**.

30. Das Flugzeug _____ gelandet.   — ist
31. Wir _____ in Leipzig gewesen.   — sind
32. Wer _____ das Auto gefahren?   — hat
33. Er _____ oft in den Alpen gewandert.   — ist
34. Er sagt, daß er mit der Straßenbahn gefahren _____.   — ist
35. Wie lange _____ Sie in Liechtenstein geblieben?   — sind
36. Was _____ passiert?   — ist
37. Wir _____ im Hotel gewohnt.   — haben
38. _____ du durch die Schweiz gereist?   — Bist
39. Nichts _____ geschehen.   — ist

4. Formation of the past participle

40. Both weak and strong verbs form their past participle with
    the prefix _____.   — **ge-**
41. Weak verbs add the ending _____.   — **-t** (or **-et**)
42. Strong verbs add the ending _____.   — **-en**
43. Strong verbs usually also change their _____ _____.   — stem vowel

*Complete with the past participle of the cue infinitive. (The past
participle vowel of strong verbs is indicated.)*

44. (sprechen, o) Ich habe oft Deutsch _____.   — gesprochen
45. (tanzen) Wo habt ihr am Wochenende _____?   — getanzt
46. (bleiben, ie) Er ist nicht lange hier _____.   — geblieben
47. (haben) Ich habe keine Zeit _____.   — gehabt
48. (fliegen, o) Wir sind mit Lufthansa _____.   — geflogen
49. (kommen, o) Wann seid ihr _____?   — gekommen
50. (lesen, e) Er will wissen, ob du die Annonce _____ hast. — gelesen
51. (laufen, au) Sie ist sehr schnell _____.   — gelaufen

5. Mixed verbs

The most common mixed verbs are:

52. *to know* (a person) _____   — **kennen**
53. *to name* _____   — **nennen**
54. *to run* _____   — **rennen**

55. *to bring* _____   — **bringen**
56. *to think* _____   — **denken**
57. *to know* (an abstraction) _____   — **wissen**
58. Mixed verbs are called "mixed" because they combine the weak ending _____ with the strong _____ _____.   — **-t**, vowel change

Complete with the past participle.

59. (denken) Das habe ich mir _____!   — gedacht
60. (bringen) Hast du das Bier _____?   — gebracht
61. (kennen) Er hat Fritz gut _____.   — gekannt
62. (wissen) Haben Sie das nicht _____?   — gewußt
63. (rennen) Er sagt, daß er heute schon _____ ist.   — gerannt
64. (nennen) Er hat mich „Dummkopf" _____!   — genannt

6. Principal parts of verbs

65. The principal parts of a verb are the _____, the _____ _____, and the _____ _____.   — infinitive, past tense, past participle

66. Vowel changes in a dictionary or a vocabulary are shown for (strong and mixed/weak) verbs.   — strong and mixed

67. A third vowel indicates that the verb also has a vowel change in the _____- and _____-forms of the (past/present) tense.   — **du, er/sie**, present

Give the principal parts indicated by the vowels.

68. finden, a, u _____ _____   — fand, gefunden

69. geben (i), a, e _____ _____ _____   — gibt, gab, gegeben

7. Separable and inseparable prefix verbs in the present perfect

70. Verbs with separable prefixes place **-ge-** between the _____ and the _____ of the past participle.   — prefix, stem

71. Verbs with inseparable prefixes (form/do not form) their past participle with **ge-**.   — do not form

72. The most common inseparable prefixes are, in alphabetical order: _____, _____, _____, _____, _____, _____, and _____.   — **be-, emp-, ent-, er-, ge-, ver-, zer-**

73. Another group of verbs that do not use the prefix **ge-** in forming the past participle are the verbs whose infinitive ends in _____.   — **-ieren**

Complete with the past participle of the cue verb.

74. (gefallen (ä), ie, a)   Fräulein Tina, Ihr Foto hat mir gut

     _____.   — gefallen
75. (aus·sehen (ie), a, e)   Wie hat er heute _____?   — ausgesehen
76. (annoncieren)   Er hat in der Zeitung _____.   — annonciert
77. (erfüllen)   Sie hat ihm den Wunsch gern(e) _____.   — erfüllt
78. (verdienen)   Wieviel Geld hast du _____?   — verdient
79. (kennen·lernen)   Wo haben Sie das Mädchen _____?   — kennengelernt
80. (akzeptieren)   Sie sagen, daß sie das nicht _____ haben. — akzeptiert
81. (studieren)   Er sagt, daß er das nicht _____ hat.   — studiert
82. (mit·nehmen (i), a, o)   Ich habe es nicht, weil sie es

     _____ hat.   — mitgenommen
83. (an·fangen (ä), i, a)   Die Vorlesung hat schon _____.   — angefangen

Restate in the present perfect.

84. Sie vergessen Ihren Regenschirm!

     _____

     _____   — Sie haben
                                                          Ihren Regenschirm
                                                          vergessen!

85. Was essen Sie?

     _____   — Was haben Sie
                                                          gegessen?

86. Du hilfst ihm. Ich weiß, daß _____

     _____   — du ihm geholfen hast.

87. Die Zeitung bringt heute schlechte Nachrichten.

     _____

     _____   — Die Zeitung hat
                                                          heute schlechte
                                                          Nachrichten
                                                          gebracht.

88. Ich stehe um acht Uhr auf.

     _____

     _____   — Ich bin um acht Uhr
                                                          aufgestanden.

89. Er zahlt die Rechnung.

_____ — Er hat die Rechnung
                                            gezahlt.

90. Wieviel Käse produziert die Schweiz?

_____

_____ — Wieviel Käse hat die
                                            Schweiz produziert?

91. Der Film gefällt mir. Ich sage, daß _____

_____ _____ _____ — mir der Film gefallen
                                        hat.

92. Wann kommen Sie an?

_____ — Wann sind Sie
                                            angekommen?

8. der-words

Some of the most common der-words are:

93. *this, that, these* _____   — **dies-**
94. *each, every* _____   — **jed-**
95. *that, those* _____   — **jen-**
96. *many a, several, some* _____   — **manch-**
97. *such, such a* _____   — **solch-**
98. *which* _____   — **welch-**

99. These determiners are known as **der**-words because they
    have the same ending as the _____ article.   — definite

Replace the definite article by the **der**-*word suggested by the cue.*

100. (*which*) Das Wort verstehen Sie nicht?
     _____ Wort verstehen Sie nicht?   — Welches
101. (*this*) Das Souvenir habe ich in Trier gekauft.
     _____ Souvenir habe ich in Trier gekauft.   — Dieses
102. (*this*) Ich wohne bei der Familie.
     Ich wohne bei _____ Familie.   — dieser
103. (*each*) Österreich gefällt dem Touristen.
     Österreich gefällt _____ Touristen.   — jedem

*Translate the **der**-word.*

104. Solche Fragen sind sehr populär. _____ *questions are very popular.*
   — *Such*
105. Manches Schulkind lernt sehr schnell lesen. _____ *schoolchild learns to read very quickly.*
   — *Many a*
106. Manche Leute wollen nie unrecht haben. _____ *people will never admit to being wrong.*
   — *Some*
107. Das weiß jedes Kind! _____ *child knows that!*
   — *Every*

9. Prepositions governing the genitive

The four main prepositions that require the use of the genitive are:

108. *instead of* _____
   — **(an)statt**
109. *in spite of* _____
   — **trotz**
110. *during* _____
   — **während**
111. *because* _____
   — **wegen**

Complete with an appropriate genitive preposition.

112. _____ der Inflation ist das Leben heute sehr teuer.
   — *Wegen*
113. Wir fahren _____ des Wochenendes nach Freiburg.
   — *während*
114. Ich möchte _____ eines Fahrrads ein Auto haben.
   — *statt*
115. _____ des Herzanfalls kann er bald wieder aufstehen.
   — *Trotz*
116. _____ des Winters wohnen wir an der Riviera.
   — *Während*

Während: *while* vs. *during*

*Give the English equivalent of **während**.*

117. Während es in Nordamerika Winter ist, ist es in Südamerika Sommer. _____
   — *While*
118. Während des Sommers ist es oft sehr heiß. _____
   — *During*

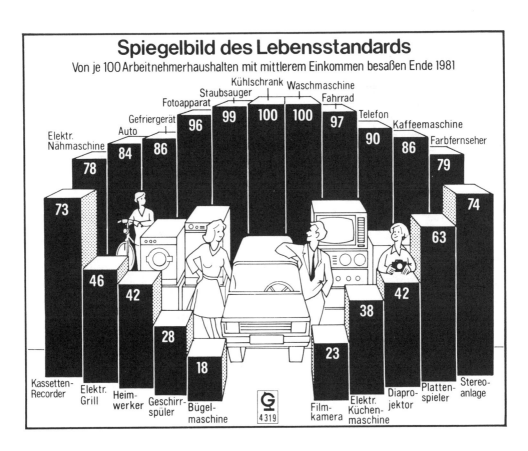

Spiegelbild des Lebensstandards
Von je 100 Arbeitnehmerhaushalten mit mittlerem Einkommen besaßen Ende 1981

Source: Inter Nationes

Erweitern Sie Ihren Wortschatz!

Englisch-Deutsch

1. television _____

2. population _____

3. proverb, saying _____

4. topic, theme _____

5. arm _____

6. energy crisis _____

7. firm, company _____

8. danger _____

9. plan _____

). married couple _____

. picture _____

. solution, answer _____

the sixties _____

14. to decrease _____

15. to think of _____

16. to discuss _____

17. to succeed _____

18. to rise, climb _____

19. to begin _____

20. some, several _____

21. every _____

22. I didn't say that, did I? _____

_____

23. we are in no hurry _____

24. to ask a question _____

25. to face a decision _____

B. Deutsch-Englisch

1. das Nullwachstum _____
2. die Tochter _____
3. der Punkt _____
4. die Zahl _____
5. der Krieg _____
6. die Wirklichkeit _____
7. der Grund _____
8. der Gastarbeiter _____
9. die Familie _____
10. der Gegner _____
11. der Herbst _____
12. das Gebiet _____
13. das Ausland _____

14. die Erde _____
15. der Enkel _____
16. mitverdienen _____
17. erreichen _____
18. stellen _____
19. führen _____
20. vergehen _____
21. letzt- _____
22. zuviel _____
23. außer Haus _____
24. immer mehr _____
25. die Milliarde _____

_____

Hör zu . . .und antworte!   Antwortbogen

Übung A. *Circle A, B, or C. Sometimes more than one answer is correct.*

1. A   B   C   2. A   B   C   3. A   B   C   4. A   B   C

5. A   B   C   6. A   B   C

Übung B. *Circle* **Logisch** *or* **Unlogisch**.

1. L   U   2. L   U   3. L   U   4. L   U   5. L   U   6. L   U

Übung C. *Circle 1, 2, or 3.*

1. 1   2   3   2. 1   2   3   3. 1   2   3   4. 1   2   3   5. 1   2   3

6. 1   2   3   7. 1   2   3   8. 1   2   3   9. 1   2   3   10. 1   2   3

Übung D. *Circle* **Richtig** *or* **Falsch**.

1. R   F   2. R   F   3. R   F   4. R   F   5. R   F   6. R   F

7. R   F   8. R   F   9. R   F   10. R   F   11. R   F   12. R   F

13. R   F   14. R   F   15. R   F

Übung **E**. *Circle 1, 2, or 3.*

1. 1   2   3   2. 1   2   3   3. 1   2   3   4. 1   2   3   5. 1   2   3

6. 1   2   3   7. 1   2   3   8. 1   2   3   9. 1   2   3   10. 1   2   3

Kapitel 8

Selbst-Test

DIALOG

Translate the underlined expressions.

1. <u>Wie hieß dieser Professor?</u>

2. Es war <u>ein Zufall</u>.
3. <u>Sie bekam</u> den Nobelpreis
4. <u>Er entdeckte</u> dieses Metall.
5. <u>Sie haben recht</u>.

— What was this professor's name?

— a coincidence
— She received
— He discovered
— You are right

1. The past tense: weak, strong, mixed verbs

6. The past tense is also known as the _____ past.
7. The past tense resembles a (snapshot/motion picture) of past events.
8. Like most English verbs, German weak verbs form their past tense with the help of a dental sound. In German, this sound is _____.
9. The personal verb endings for weak verbs in the past tense are -e- for the _____ and _____ forms;
10. -en for the _____ and _____ forms;
11. -est for the _____ form;
12. -et for the _____ form.
13. A linking -e- is inserted to make the past tense dental sound audible when the verb stem ends in _____ or _____, as well as in _____ or _____.

— narrative

— motion picture

— -t-

— ich-, er/sie-
— wir-, sie/Sie-
— du-
— ihr-

— -d, -t, -m, -n

Give the past tense forms.

14. ich, er/sie entdeck___
15. wir, sie/Sie entdeck___
16. du entdeck___

— -te
— -ten
— -test

17. ihr entdeck___   — -tet

18. ich, er/sie arbeit___   — -ete

19. wir, sie/Sie arbeit___   — -eten

20. du arbeit___   — -etest

21. ihr arbeit___   — -etet

22. Strong verbs form their past tense by changing the _____
    _____.   — stem vowel

23. The personal endings for strong verbs are (the same as/different from) those of weak verbs, but there is no ending in the _____ and _____ forms.   — the same as, ich-, er-

24. When the stem ends in _____ or _____, a linking _____ is inserted.   — -d, -t, -e-

Supply the past tense ending, if one is necessary.

       geben *to give*

25. ich, er/sie gab___   — no ending

26. wir, sie/Sie gab___   — -en

27. du gab___   — -st

28. ihr gab___   — -t

       finden *to find*

29. ich, er/sie fand___   — no ending

30. wir, sie/Sie fand___   — -en

31. du fand___   — -est

32. ihr fand___   — -et

33. Although the vowel change cannot be predicted, many German strong verbs follow the same vowel-change pattern as their _____ cognates.   — English

Give the principal parts of the German equivalent.

34. *come, came, come* _____, _____, _____   — kommen, kam, gekommen

35. *drink, drank, drunk* _____, _____, _____   — trinken, trank, getrunken

36. Some strong verbs change not only the stem vowel, but the entire _____.   — stem

Give the past tense **er**-*form of the verb.*

37. gehen   er _____   — ging

38. stehen   er _____   — stand

39. tun   er _____   — tat

40. The vowel change in the past tense is (always/not necessarily) maintained in the past participle.   — not necessarily

Complete, changing the verb from the present to the past tense.

41. Ich warte auf dich. Ich _____ auf dich.   — wartete
42. Wir antworten dir. Wir _____ dir.   — antworteten
43. Was sagt er? Was _____ er?   — sagte
44. Wieviel kostet es? Wieviel _____ es?   — kostete
45. Sie verkaufen es. Sie _____ es.   — verkauften
46. Wann besuchst du ihn? Wann _____ du ihn?   — besuchtest
47. Ich brauche viel Geld. Ich _____ viel Geld.   — brauchte

Supply the past tense of the cue verb.

48. (fahren (ä), u, a) Viele Deutsche _____ ans Meer.   — fuhren
49. (treffen (i), a, o) Überall _____ man deutsche Touristen.   — traf
50. (geben (i), a, e) Es _____ viele Charterflüge.   — gab
51. (ankommen, a, o) Gestern _____ viele Touristen _____.   — kamen . . . an
52. (schreiben, ie, ie) Ich _____ an das Reisebüro.   — schrieb
53. (sprechen (i), a, o) _____ ihr immer nur Deutsch?   — Spracht
54. (stehen, a, a) Was _____ in der Zeitung?   — stand

55. Mixed verbs form their past tense both by a change in the
_____ _____ and with the help of the dental sound _____.   — stem vowel, -t-

Give the past tense.

56. denken   ich _____   — dachte
57. rennen   du _____   — ranntest
58. bringen   wir _____   — brachten
59. wissen   er _____   — wußte
60. kennen   ihr _____   — kanntet
61. nennen   sie (*she*) _____   — nannte

Give the past tense form of **haben,** **sein,** *and* **werden.**

haben

62. ich, er _____   — hatte
63. du _____   — hattest
64. wir, sie/Sie _____   — hatten
65. ihr _____   — hattet

sein

66. ich, er _____   — war
67. du _____   — warst
68. wir, sie/Sie _____   — waren
69. ihr _____   — wart

werden

70. ich, er _____   — wurde

71. du _____   — wurdest
72. wir, sie/Sie _____   — wurden
73. ihr _____   — wurdet

Restate in the past tense or in the present perfect.

74. Ich habe hier gestanden. Ich _____.   — stand hier

75. Er rief uns an. Er _____.   — hat uns angerufen

2. The past tense of modals

Supply the past tense of the cue modal.

76. (müssen) Ich _____ es tun.   — mußte
77. (dürfen) Wir _____ nach Hause gehen.   — durften
78. (können) Warum _____ du nicht kommen?   — konntest
79. (sollen) Er _____ gestern mitkommen.   — sollte
80. (wollen) _____ Sie es nicht kaufen?   — Wollten

81. Three of the above modals form their past tense like mixed
    verbs. They are: _____, _____, and _____.   **— dürfen, können,**
                                                        müssen

82. The vowel change they undergo consists of (umlauting/
    dropping the umlaut).   — dropping the umlaut

83. The modals that undergo no change in the stem vowel are
    _____ and _____.   **— sollen, wollen**

Complete the German equivalent.

84. *I had to see it.* Ich _____.   — mußte es sehen

85. *He was allowed to do it.* Er _____.   — durfte es tun

86. A separable prefix verb follows the same word-order pattern
    in the past tense as in the _____ tense.   — present
87. In a main clause, the prefix is (separated/not separated). — separated
88. In a dependent clause, the prefix (is separated from/remains
    attached to) the verb stem.   — remains attached to

Restate in the past tense.

89. Er steht jeden Tag um sieben auf.

    Er _____.   — stand jeden Tag um
                                                          sieben auf

90. Ich weiß, daß er immer um sechs aufsteht.

    Ich _____.

        — weiß, daß er immer um sechs aufstand

Arrange the cue words into a sentence in the past tense.

91. (anrufen/er/heute) _____

        — Er rief heute an.

92. (anrufen/er/gestern) Er sagt, daß _____.

        — er gestern anrief

3. Uses of the infinitive

93. In a main clause, the complementary infinitive of a modal stands (at the end/next to the end) of the clause.

        — at the end

94. In a dependent clause, the sequence is (modal-infinitive/infinitive-modal).

        — infinitive-modal

Give the German equivalent.

95. *He wants to excavate Troy.*

    _____

        — Er will Troja ausgraben.

96. *He says that he wants to excavate Troy.*

    _____

        — Er sagte, daß er Troja ausgraben will.

Other verbs used with the infinitive are:

97. *to help* _____   — helfen
98. *to hear* _____   — hören
99. *to let* _____   — lassen
100. *to learn* _____   — lernen
101. *to see* _____   — sehen

Give the German equivalent.

102. *I hear the train coming.*

    Ich . . . den Zug . . . _____

        — höre . . . kommen.

103. *He does not let me speak.*

    Er . . . mich nicht . . . _____

        — Er läßt . . . sprechen.

Translate.

104. Professor Röntgen mußte auch lehren.

— *Professor Röntgen also had to teach*

105. Frau Schliemann half Troja finden.

— *Mrs. Schliemann helped to find Troja.*

106. Ich weiß, daß Frau von Suttner gegen den Krieg protestieren

wollte. _____

— *I know that Mrs. Suttner wanted to protest against war.*

107. Man läßt uns hier nicht parken.

_____

— *One does not let us park here.*

108. Wir lassen uns einen VW aus Deutschland kommen.

_____

— *We are having a VW shipped from Germany.*

109. Ich konnte das Telefon nicht hören.

_____

— *I was not able to hear the telephone.*

4. ein-words and possessive adjectives

The possessive adjectives are:

110. *my* _____, *your* (familiar) _____, *his* _____
111. *her* _____, *our* _____, *your* (familiar plural) _____
112. *their* _____, *your* (formal) _____

— **mein, dein, sein**
— **ihr, unser, euer**
— **ihr, Ihr**

113. The possessive adjectives are called **ein**-words because they have the same endings as _____ and _____.

— **ein, kein**

114. The possessive adjective has the same gender, number and case as the _____ which follows.

— noun

Supply the cue possessive adjective.

115. (mein) Das ist _____ Mann.
116. (mein) Das ist _____ Frau.
117. (mein) Das ist _____ Auto.

— mein
— meine
— mein

Supply the proper ending, if one is necessary.

DATIVE
118. Ich gebe es mein___ Mann.

— -em

119. Ich gebe es mein___ Frau.   — -er
120. Ich gebe es uns___ Kind.   — -(e)rem

ACCUSATIVE
121. Ich sehe dein___ Mann.   — -en
122. Ich sehe dein___ Frau.   — -e
123. Ich sehe uns___ Auto.   — -er

GENITIVE
124. Wo ist das Foto Ihr___ Mannes?   — -es
125. Wo ist das Foto Ihr___ Frau?   — -er
126. Wo ist das Foto eur___ Kindes?   — -es

NOMINATIVE
127. Hier kommt Ihr___ Mann.   — no ending
128. Hier kommt Ihr___ Frau.   — -e
129. Hier kommt Ihr___ Kind.   — no ending

130. The gender and case of the possessive adjective are determined by the _____ it modifies, but the choice of **sein**
(*masculine*) or **ihr** (*feminine*) is determined by the _____.   — noun, possessor

Supply the appropriate form of **sein** *or* **ihr.**

131. Herr Stern und _____ Sohn sind hier.   — sein
132. Herr Stern und _____ Tochter sind hier.   — seine
133. Frau Stern und _____ Sohn sind hier.   — ihr
134. Frau Stern und _____ Tochter sind hier.   — ihre
135. Erika und _____ Bruder helfen uns.   — ihr
136. Fritz und _____ Bruder helfen uns.   — sein
137. Erika und _____ Schwester helfen uns.   — ihre
138. Fritz und _____ Schwester helfen uns.   — seine
139. Tina gab mir _____ Auto.   — ihr
140. Kurt gab mir _____ Auto.   — sein

Complete with the German equivalent of the cue.

141. (*my*) Geben Sie mir _____ Koffer, bitte!   — meinen
142. (*my*) Was machen Sie mit _____ Koffer?   — meinem
143. (*her*) Was ist die Nummer von _____ Zimmer?   — ihrem
144. (*your*) Was schreiben Sie _____ Tochter?   — Ihrer
145. (*your*) Siehst du oft _____ Bruder?   — deinen
146. (*your*, formal) Ich kenne _____ Mann sehr gut.   — Ihren
147. (*our*) Sehen Sie _____ Wagen?   — uns(e)ren
148. (*your*, formal) Was ist die Adresse _____ Arztes?   — Ihres

Replace the possessive adjective by the indefinite article and vice versa. Note the similar ending.

149. Das ist das Auto von meinem Studenten.
     Das ist das Auto von _____ Studenten.   — einem
150. Hier ist die Adresse einer Apotheke.
     (*our*) Hier ist die Adresse _____ Apotheke.   — uns(e)rer
151. Ich sehe keinen Wagen hier.
     (*her*) Ich sehe _____ Wagen hier.   — ihren

Translate.

152. *I know him.* _____   — Ich kenne ihn.
153. *I can do it.* _____   — Ich kann es tun.
154. *We know it.* _____   — Wir wissen es.
155. *We know her.* _____   — Wir kennen sie.
156. *We can see it.* _____   — Wir können es sehen.
157. *I know German.* _____   — Ich kann Deutsch.

5. Months of the year, seasons

Complete the sentence.

158. Viele Leute heiraten im _____.   — Frühling (*or* Juni)
159. Der Monat Dezember ist im _____.   — Winter
160. Das Herbstsemester fängt im _____ an.   — September
161. Memorial Day ist im Monat _____.   — Mai
162. Thanksgiving ist im Monat _____.   — November
163. Der Winter hört im Monat _____ auf.   — März

With kind permission of Herr Tetsche and *Stern Magazin*, No. 30, 1982

Probe-Test

A. *Translate the underlined expressions.*

1. <u>Als sein Chef</u> einmal <u>sah</u>, daß er eine schöne Handschrift hatte, <u>machte er ihn</u> zum Schreiber.

   _____

2. <u>Als sein Bruder starb, ging er nach Amerika.</u> _____

   _____

3. <u>Bald wurde er Millionär.</u> _____

4. <u>Eines Morgens fand Schliemann</u> einen großen Topf. _____

5. <u>Wem gehörten</u> diese wunderbaren Schätze? _____

B. *Complete.*

1. The characteristic signal for the past tense of weak verbs is _____.

2. The _____ and _____ forms of strong verbs never have an ending in the past tense.

3. Some modals have a vowel change in the past tense. An example is the infinitive

   _____, which becomes **ich** _____ in the past.

4. Verbs with separable prefixes follow the same pattern of word order in the past tense as in the

   _____ tense.

C. *Complete the German equivalent.*

1. *I had time.* Ich _____ Zeit.

2. *Fritz, were you at home?* Fritz, _____ du zu Hause?

3. *He got rich quickly.* Er _____ schnell reich.

4. *She ran home.* Sie _____ nach Hause.

5. *Did you know that?* _____ Sie das?

6. *He opened the door.* Er _____ die Tür.

7. *We worked a lot.* Wir _____ viel.

8. *He stood here.* Er _____ hier.

9. *They went away.* Sie _____ fort.

10. *Did he come along?* _____ er _____ ?

11. *We spoke about him.* Wir _____ über ihn.

12. *I thought so, too.* Ich _____ auch so.

13. *I had to do it.* Ich _____ es tun.

14. *When did you want to leave?* Wann _____ du abfahren?

15. *He discovered it.* Er _____ es.

16. *She received the Nobel Prize.* Sie _____ den Nobelpreis.

D. *Complete with the cue sentence.*

1. (Schliemann grub Troja aus.) Ich weiß, daß _____

2. (Schliemann grub Troja aus.) Wann _____ ?

3. (Schliemann wollte Troja ausgraben.) Ich weiß, daß_____

_____

4. (Schliemann will Troja ausgraben.) Die Zeitung schreibt, daß _____

_____

E. *Arrange the cue words in their proper word order. Write your sentences in* a) *the present tense, and* b) *the past tense.*

(sparen/wir/können/kein Geld)

1. a) _____.

   b) _____.

2. a) Ich weiß, daß _____.

   b) Ich weiß, daß _____.

F. 1. Some of the verbs that can take an infinitive, besides the modals, are

_____, _____, _____.

G. *Translate.*

1. Mit den Strahlen kann man das Herz sehen. _____.

2. Wir durften Fritz im Krankenhaus besuchen. _____.

H. *Complete with the German equivalent of the cue word.*

1. (*my*) Wo ist _____ Taxi?

2. (*her*) Ich brauche _____ Adresse.

3. (*your*, familiar) Ich spreche mit _____ Freund.

4. (*your*, formal) Er spricht mit _____ Freundin.

5. (*our*) Nach _____ Ferien war das Wetter wieder schön.

6. (*her*) Was ist die Adresse _____ Ärztin?

7. (*his*) Er kommt mit _____ Sohn.

8. (*her*) Sie kommt mit _____ Bruder.

9. (*her*) Er kommt mit _____ Schwester.

10. (*your*) Wer ist _____ Lehrer, Karl?

11. (*your*) Was schreiben Sie _____ Bruder, Herr Schwarz?

12. (*his*) Er wohnt bei _____ Eltern.

13. (*our*) Das Geld ist für _____ Sohn.

I. *Translate.*

1. *We know her.* _____

2. *We knew it.* _____

3. *I know German.* _____

J. *Complete with the correct choice.*

1. Man fand (Geschichten/Mauern/Sagen) _____, genau wie Homer sie

   (beschrieb/lernte/gründete) _____.

2. Man grub (größer/schöner/tiefer) _____ in den (Topf/Hügel/Handel)

   _____.

3. Über Schliemanns (Theorien/Werkzeuge/Spuren) _____ haben

   Wissenschaftler (bewiesen/diskutiert/verdient) _____.

4. Flohen die Trojaner nicht aus einer (brennenden/erfundenen/ausgegrabenen)

   _____ Stadt?

Erweitern Sie Ihren Wortschatz!

A. Englisch-Deutsch

1. discovery _____
2. name _____
3. trade _____
4. story; history _____
5. hour _____
6. worker _____
7. month _____
8. book _____
9. foreign language _____
10. peace _____
11. weapon _____
12. to receive _____
13. to tell _____

14. to follow _____
15. to die _____
16. to leave _____
17. to come back _____
18. nobody _____
19. wonderful _____
20. hundred _____
21. famous _____
22. deep _____
23. finally _____
24. unknown _____
   _____
25. that's right _____

B. Deutsch-Englisch

1. der Hügel _____

2. der Tip _____

3. der Strahl _____

4. der Zufall _____

5. der Fluß _____

6. der Chef _____

7. der Erfolg _____

8. der Staatsbürger _____

9. das Messer _____

10. der Bruder _____

11. die Mauer _____

12. der Dichter _____

13. das Studium _____

14. entdecken _____

15. beweisen _____

16. übernehmen _____

17. faszinieren _____

18. nieder _____

19. arm _____

20. als _____

21. noch einmal _____

22. achtjährig _____

23. eines Tages _____

24. noch mehr _____

25. eigen _____

Hör zu . . .und antworte!   Antwortbogen

Übung A. *Circle* **Richtig** *or* **Falsch.**

1. R F   2. R F   3. R F   4. R F   5. R F   6. R F

7. R F   8. R F   9. R F   10. R F   11. R F   12. R F

Übung B. *Circle 1, 2, or 3.*

1. 1 2 3   2. 1 2 3   3. 1 2 3   4. 1 2 3   5. 1 2 3

6. 1 2 3   7. 1 2 3   8. 1 2 3   9. 1 2 3   10. 1 2 3

Übung C. *Circle 1, 2, or 3.*

1. 1 2 3   2. 1 2 3   3. 1 2 3   4. 1 2 3   5. 1 2 3

6. 1 2 3   7. 1 2 3   8. 1 2 3   9. 1 2 3   10. 1 2 3

Übung D. *Circle A, B, or C. More than one answer may be correct.*

1. A B C   2. A B C   3. A B C   4. A B C

5. A B C   6. A B C   7. A B C   8. A B C

9. A B C   10. A B C   11. A B C   12. A B C

13. A B C   14. A B C   15. A B C   16. A B C

Kapitel 9

Selbst-Test

DIALOG

Translate the underlined expressions.

1. <u>Davon habe ich schon gehört</u>. — I heard about it already.

2. <u>Da irrst du dich</u>. — There you are wrong.
3. Tennis <u>kann ich mir nicht leisten</u>. — I can't afford (for myself)

4. Damit habe ich in Deutschland <u>angefangen</u>. — I began with it
5. <u>Er ist seit zwei Wochen hier</u>. — He's been here for two weeks.

1. da-compounds

6. The **da**-compound is a combination of **da** and a _____. — preposition
7. Equivalents of German **da**-compounds also occur in English, but mostly in _____ language. — legal
8. The German equivalent for *therein* is _____; for *thereto*, it is _____. — **darin, dazu**
9. A linking **-r-** is inserted between **da** and the preposition when the latter begins with a _____. — vowel
10. The **da**-compounds are (never/sometimes) used to refer to human beings. — never
11. They are used to refer to an _____ thing or a _____. — inanimate, concept

*Answer with a **da**-compound or a preposition and a personal pronoun, whichever is appropriate.*

12. Sprecht ihr über die Entdeckung Trojas? Ja, wir sprechen _____. — darüber
13. Sprecht ihr über Schliemann? Ja, wir sprechen _____. — über ihn

14. Wer erzählte Heinrich die Sage von Troja? Sein Vater erzählte ihm _____.

    — davon

15. Hörte er die Sage zuerst von seinem Vater? Ja, er hörte sie zuerst _____.

    — von ihm

16. Was wollte Professor Röntgen mit seiner Entdeckung machen? Er wollte _____ den Menschen helfen.

    — damit

Complete with a **da**-*compound or a preposition and a personal pronoun, whichever is appropriate.*

17. Seine Frau half ihm bei der Ausgrabung. Seine Frau half ihm _____.

    — dabei

18. Sie blieb immer bei ihrem Mann. Sie blieb immer _____.

    — bei ihm

19. Durch seine Ausgrabung hat er seine Theorie bewiesen. _____ hat er seine Theorie bewiesen.

    — Dadurch

20. Viele Wissenschaftler waren gegen seine Theorie. Viele Wissenschaftler waren _____.

    — dagegen

21. Viele Wissenschaftler waren gegen Schliemann. Viele Wissenschaftler waren _____.

    — gegen ihn

22. When **damit** is used as a subordinating conjunction, it corresponds to English _____, and not to _____.

    — *so that, therewith (with it)*

Complete with the English equivalent of the underlined words.

23. Er spielt oft damit. *He often plays* _____.

    — *with it*

24. Damit Sie es wissen! Sie haben sich geirrt! _____ *You were wrong!*

    — *So that you know it!*

25. Ich rauche nicht, damit ich gesund bleibe. *I don't smoke _____.*

    — *so that I remain healthy*

2. wo-compounds

26. The **wo**-compound is only used when referring to things or ideas, and in _____.

    — questions

27. It is never used to refer to _____ _____.

    — human beings

28. For persons, a preposition plus **wer**, _____, _____, or _____ is used, depending on the case.

    — **wen, wem, wessen**

Complete with the appropriate **wo**-*compound or preposition plus the personal question word, whichever is appropriate.*

29. (aus der Stadt) _____ flohen die Trojaner?

    — Woraus

30. (vor den Griechen) _____ flohen die Trojaner?

    — Vor wem

31. (Schliemann erzählte von Troja) _____ erzählte er?

    — Wovon

32. (die Leute diskutierten über seine Theorie) _____
    diskutierten die Leute?   — Worüber
33. (mit seiner Frau) _____ grub er den Schatz aus?   — Mit wem
34. (auf den Mauern) _____ konnte man die Spuren eines Brandes sehen? — Worauf
35. (auf seine Frau) _____ wartet Schliemann?   — Auf wen

36. **Da**-compounds are also used to refer to an idea that (has
    already been/will be/has already been or will be) expressed.   — has already been or
         will be

37. These are known as _____ and _____ da-compounds.   — anticipatory,
         retrospective

Complete the English equivalent.

38. Daß Homers Sage wahr war, daran zweifelte Schliemann nie.
    That Homer's saga was true, _____.   — *Schliemann never*
         doubted

39. Viele Leute zweifelten daran, daß Homers Sage wahr war.
    _____ *that Homer's saga was true.*   — *Many people*
         doubted

40. In which of the two preceding items does the **da**-compound
    anticipate what will be expressed? _____   — No. 39

Give the English equivalent.

41. Woran denken Sie? _____   — *What are you*
         thinking about?
42. Worauf warten Sie? _____   — *What are you waiting*
         for?
43. Wozu brauchst du das? _____   — *What do you need*
         this for?
44. Worauf freust du dich? _____   — *What are you looking*
         forward to?

3. Reflexive pronouns

45. In a reflexive sentence, the subject and the _____ are the
    same.   — object
46. What is the subject? *Eva combs her hair.* **Eva kämmt sich.**
    _____   — **Eva**
47. What is the object of the preceding sentence? _____   — **sich**
48. Except for **sich**, the forms of the reflexive pronoun in the
    dative and accusative are the same as those of the _____
    pronoun.   — personal
49. **Sich** is used with **er**/**du**, **sie** *she*/**ich**, **Sie** *you*/**ihr** *you*,
    and **sie** *they*/**wir**.   — **er, sie, Sie, sie**

50. The difference between the accusative and the dative (is/ is not) apparent in all forms of the reflexive pronoun. — is not

51. The forms of the reflexive pronoun are different in the accusative and dative only in the _____ and _____ forms. **— ich-, du-**

52. The dative reflexive is generally used when there is an additional (direct/indirect) object, or when the verb requires a (dative/accusative) object. — direct, dative

Give the dative and accusative objects.

53. **Ich kämme mir das Haar.**
accusative _____, dative _____ **— das Haar, mir**

4. Reflexive verbs

54. A verb may change its _____ when used reflexively. — meaning
55. Some verbs must _____ be used with the reflexive pronoun. — always

Supply the appropriate accusative or dative reflexive pronoun.

56. Er kauft _____ ein Auto. — sich
57. Ich irre _____ nie. — mich
58. Er rasiert _____. — sich
59. Wofür interessierst du _____? — dich
60. Kämm _____ doch das Haar! — dir
61. Wir treffen _____ um fünf Uhr. — uns
62. Ich kann _____ das nicht leisten. — mir
63. Identifiziert _____! — euch
64. Fühlst du _____ nicht wohl? — dich
65. Beeilen Sie _____! — sich
66. Hier hat _____ nicht viel geändert. — sich
67. Wann hast du _____ erkältet? — dich

Complete the translation.

68. Ich erinnere mich an ihn. *I _____.* — *remember him*
69. Ich erinnere Sie daran. *I _____.* — *remind you of it*
70. Wann ziehst du um? *When _____?* — *are you moving*
71. Warum ziehst du dich um? *Why _____?* — *are you changing (clothes)*

Complete with the new subject.

72. Wascht euch! (du) Wasch _____! — dich
73. Ich muß mich beeilen. Wir _____. — müssen uns beeilen
74. Er duscht sich. Ich _____. — dusche mich
75. Zieht sie sich an? (ihr) _____? — Zieht ihr euch an?

5. Definite and indefinite time

76. Definite time is expressed by the _____ case.   — accusative

77. Indefinite time is expressed by the _____ case.   — genitive

Supply the German equivalent.

78. *Some day I'll visit you.* _____ besuche ich dich.   — Eines Tages

79. *I see her every day.* Ich sehe sie _____.   — jeden Tag

80. *They go to Europe every year.* Sie fahren _____ nach
Europa.   — jedes Jahr

81. *I usually jog in the morning.* Ich laufe gewöhnlich _____.   — morgens

6. seit: past time continued into the present

82. **Seit** is used to express an action that began in the _____ but
is still going on in the _____.   — past, present

Translate.

83. Er ist seit sechs Jahren verheiratet. _____   — *He has been married
for six years.*

84. Seit gestern ist das Wetter wieder schön. _____   — *Since yesterday the
weather has been
nice again.*

85. Instead of **seit,** the adverb _____, followed by an expression
of time in the accusative, may be used.   — **schon**

*Complete, using **schon** to express the same idea.*

86. Ich warte seit zehn Minuten auf dich! Ich warte _____!   — schon zehn Minuten
auf dich

Erweitern Sie Ihren Wortschatz!

A. Englisch-Deutsch

1. university _____

2. week _____

3. cold _____

4. woods, forest _____

5. beginner _____

6. government _____

7. group _____

8. pupil (female) _____

9. winner, victor _____

10. dormitory _____

11. health _____

12. mixture _____

13. government _____

14. to take a shower _____

15. to be mistaken _____

16. to change, alter _____

17. to participate _____

18. to train, practice _____

19. to sleep _____

20. to run, jog _____

21. since _____

22. during _____

23. every day _____

24. It's great fun! _____

25. from top to bottom _____

_____

B. Deutsch-Englisch

1. die Sache _____

2. das Mittel _____

3. der Trimm-dich-Pfad _____

4. der Liegestütz _____

5. die Erziehung _____

6. die Mischung _____

7. der Wettkampf _____

8. das Spiel _____

9. der Held _____

10. das Alter _____

11. sich rasieren _____

12. erfinden _____

13. anschauen _____

14. finanzieren _____

15. sich interessieren _____

16. turnen _____

17. unterscheiden _____

18. feiern _____

19. verbinden _____

20. öffentlich _____

21. nachmittags _____

22. dahinter _____

23. dreimal _____

24. langweilig _____

25. ich kann es mir nicht leisten _____

_____

Hör zu . . . und antworte!   Antwortbogen

Übung **A**.   *Circle A, B, or C. Sometimes more than one answer is correct.*

1. A B C   2. A B C   3. A B C   4. A B C

5. A B C   6. A B C   7. A B C   8. A B C

9. A B C   10. A B C   11. A B C   12. A B C

Übung **B**.   *Circle A, B, or C. Sometimes more than one answer is correct.*

1. A B C   2. A B C   3. A B C   4. A B C

5. A B C   6. A B C   7. A B C   8. A B C

9. A B C   10. A B C   11. A B C   12. A B C

13. A B C

Übung **C**.   *Circle A or B or both.*

1. A B   2. A B   3. A B   4. A B   5. A B   6. A B

Übung **D.**   *Circle A, B, or C.*

1. A   B   C   2. A   B   C   3. A   B   C   4. A   B   C

5. A   B   C   6. A   B   C   7. A   B   C   8. A   B   C

9. A   B   C   10. A   B   C

Kapitel 10

Selbst-Test

DIALOG

Translate the underlined expressions.

1. <u>Was wird</u> das 21. Jahrhundert <u>bringen</u>?   — what will bring
2. Die Menschen <u>werden</u> mehr Zeit <u>haben</u>.   — will have
3. Ich glaube, <u>daß das Leben besser werden wird</u>.   — that life will become better
4. Ich dachte nicht, <u>daß Sie</u> so pessimistisch <u>sein würden</u>. — that you would be
5. <u>Als ich</u> Ihre Frage <u>hörte</u>, dachte ich . . .   — when I heard
6. <u>Wenn's</u> ein 21. Jahrhundert <u>geben wird</u> . . .   -- if there will be

1. The future tense

7. The future tense is formed by combining the present tense of _____ with an _____.   — **werden**, infinitive
8. In a main clause in the future tense, the infinitive goes (to the end/before the auxiliary).   — to the end
9. When the future tense is used with a modal, the infinitive of the _____ stands at the end.   — modal
10. When the future tense is used in a dependent clause, the final position is occupied by the conjugated form of _____.   — **werden**

Complete in the future tense.

11. Elke macht ihren ersten Besuch beim Sportklub. Elke _____ ihren ersten Besuch beim Sportklub _____.   — wird, machen
12. Eine Freundin bringt sie zum Trainer. Eine Freundin _____.   — wird sie zum Trainer bringen

13. Du wirst eine gute Schwimmerin. Du _____.

— wirst eine gute Schwimmerin werden

14. Sind meine Hände nicht zu klein? _____ meine Hände nicht größer _____?

— werden, werden

15. Er sagt, daß der Staat den Sport fördert. Er sagt, daß _____.

— der Staat den Sport fördern wird

16. Der echte Amateur muß alles selbst bezahlen. Der echte Amateur _____ alles selbst _____ _____.

— wird, bezahlen müssen

17. Elke kann heute wieder schwimmen. Elke _____.

— wird heute wieder schwimmen können

18. Die besten Sportler kommen in spezielle Sportschulen. Wir wollen wissen, ob die besten _____.

— Sportler in spezielle Sportschulen kommen werden

19. The present tense (can/cannot) be used to express future time.

— can

20. If it is used to express future time, it is used with an expression that denotes _____ time.

— future

Express future time by expanding the statement with the cue expression.

21. (morgen) Ich spiele Tennis. _____

— Ich spiele morgen Tennis.

22. (in fünf Minuten) Ich weiß, daß er hier ist. Ich weiß, daß _____.

— er in fünf Minuten hier ist

English *will* and German **will**

23. The German verb form **will** is derived from _____ (English _____).

— **wollen**, *to want to*

24. English *will*, on the other hand, is the _____ for the English future tense.

— auxiliary

*Supply the proper form of **wollen** or **werden**.*

25. *I will visit you.* Ich _____ dich besuchen.

— werde

26. *What do you want?* Was _____ Sie?   — wollen
27. *What does she want?* Was _____ sie?   — will
28. *They will buy it.* Sie _____ es kaufen.   — werden
29. *I don't want to see it.* Ich _____ es nicht sehen.   — will

2. The three functions of **werden**

30. The basic meaning of **werden** is _____.   — *to become*
31. When combined with an infinitive, **werden** signals the _____ tense.   — *future*
32. When combined with a past participle, **werden** signals the _____ voice.   — *passive*

Translate the underlined expressions.

33. Elke <u>wird</u> nie krank. *Elke never _____ sick.*   — *gets*
34. Elke <u>wird</u> Siegerin <u>werden</u>. *Elke _____ _____ a champion.*   — *will be* (or *will become*)
35. Meine Eltern _____ kommen. *My parents _____ come.*   — *will*
36. In einem kleinen Geschäft <u>wird</u> der Einkauf zu einer gesellschaftlichen Funktion. *In a small store, shopping _____ a social function.*   — *becomes*
37. In der Zukunft <u>wird</u> man alles im Supermarkt <u>kaufen</u> <u>müssen</u>. *In the future, one _____ _____ _____ _____ everything in the supermarket.*   — *will have to buy*

3. **würde**: the subjunctive form of **werden**

38. Any form of **würde** always corresponds to English _____.   — *would*

Translate.

39. Das werde ich gern(e) tun. _____   — *I'll gladly do that.*
40. Das würde ich gern(e) tun. _____   — *I would gladly do that.*
41. Würden Sie mich bitte anrufen? _____   — *Would you please call me?*
42. Wirst du mir helfen? _____   — *Will you help me?*
43. Würdest du mir helfen? _____   — *Would you help me?*

4. als, wenn, and wann

44. **Als, wenn**, and **wann** correspond to English _____. — *when*
45. In German, **als** signals an event in the (future/past). — *past*
46. **Wenn** signals (an *"if*-situation"/a repeated event/an *"if*-situation" and a repeated event). — an *"if*-situation" and a repeated event
47. **Wann** signals a (condition/question). — *question*
48. When **als** causes V-L order, it always corresponds to English _____. — *when*
49. When **als** does not produce V-L word order, it corresponds to English _____ or *than*. — *as*

Complete with als, wenn, *or* wann.

50. Wir fahren immer in die Berge, _____ das Wetter schön ist. — wenn
51. _____ fahren Sie in die Berge? — Wann
52. _____ das Wetter schön ist, bleiben wir noch einen Tag hier. — Wenn
53. _____ wir in den Bergen waren, regnete es fast jeden Tag. — Als
54. Und was machen wir, _____ das Wetter nicht schön ist? — wenn
55. Er arbeitet _____ Hotelportier in der Schweiz. — als
56. _____ warst du zum letzten Mal in der Schweiz? — Wann
57. In der Schweiz gibt es mehr hohe Berge _____ in Deutschland. — als

5. Adjectival endings: a preview

58. German distinguishes between two types of adjectives: _____ and _____. — limiting, descriptive
59. A (limiting/descriptive) adjective is also called an attributive adjective. — descriptive
60. When a descriptive adjective (precedes/follows) the noun it modifies, it has no ending. — follows
61. When the adjective follows the noun, it is often used with the verbs *to be* _____, *to become* _____, *to remain* _____, and *to seem* _____. — **sein, werden, bleiben, scheinen**
62. The definite and indefinite articles are (limiting/descriptive) adjectives. — limiting
63. Other limiting adjectives are all the **der**-words and _____-words. — **ein**

6. Descriptive adjectives following **der** and **ein**

64. The ending of a descriptive adjective that precedes the noun depends on whether the adjective is preceded by a _____ article or by an _____ article.

— definite, indefinite

65. Adjective endings that show number, gender, or case are called _____ or _____ endings.

— primary, strong

66. Adjective endings that do not necessarily reveal number, gender, or case are called _____ or _____ endings.

— secondary, weak

Indicate by the letters P *and* S *whether the underlined word has a primary or a secondary ending. If it has no ending, write* Ø .

67. ein <u>gro</u>ßes Haus ____ ____   das <u>gro</u>ße Haus ____ ____   — Ø , P; P, S
68. der <u>alte</u> Mann ____ ____   ein <u>alter</u> Mann ____ ____   — P, S; Ø, P
69. die <u>junge</u> Frau ____ ____   eine <u>junge</u> Frau ____ ____   — P, S; P, S
70. den <u>jungen</u> Mann ____ ____   der <u>jungen</u> Frau ____ ____   — P, S; P, S
71. dem <u>jungen</u> Mann ____ ____   dem <u>jungen</u> Mädchen ____ ____   — P, S; P, S

72. The basic concept is that either the limiting adjective or the descriptive adjective preceding a noun must show a _____ ending.

— primary

73. Whether preceded by a **der**-word or an **ein**-word, the ending of an adjective is always **-en** in the following cases:
   a) all (singular/plural) cases;
   b) all _____ cases, singular and plural;
   c) all _____ cases, singular and plural.

— plural
— dative
— genitive

74. The ending **-e** always occurs in the feminine singular, _____ and _____ cases, regardless of whether **die** or **eine** precedes the descriptive adjective.

— nominative, accusative

75. The three situations in which a choice between two endings has to be made are the masculine singular _____ case; the _____ singular nominative case; and the neuter singular _____ case.

— nominative, neuter, accusative

76. The choice of endings depends on whether the descriptive adjective is preceded by a _____-word or an _____-word.

— **der, ein**

77. The choice in these three situations is between the endings _____, _____, or _____.

— **-e, -er, -es**

Complete with the correct adjectival ending, if one is necessary.

78. Das ist der gut___ Wein.   — -e
79. Hier ist ein gut___ Wein.   — -er

80. Dieser Wein ist gut _____.   — no ending
81. Wo ist die neu___ Jugendherberge?   — -e
82. Gibt es hier eine neu___ Jugendherberge?   — -e
83. Diese Jugendherberge scheint neu___ zu sein.   — no ending
84. Gibt es nur dieses billig___ Zimmer?   — -e
85. Wo finde ich ein billig___ Zimmer?   — -es
86. Das Zimmer wird nicht billig___ sein.   — no ending
87. Wir haben einen schön___ Campingplatz.   — -en
88. Kennen Sie diesen schön___ Campingplatz?   — -en
89. Wir suchen eine billig___ Wohnung.   — -e
90. Seit wann haben Sie diese billig___ Wohnung?   — -e
91. Kennst du dieses klein _____ Haus?   — -e
92. Wir haben ein klein _____ Haus gefunden.   — -es
93. Wir wohnen in einem neu___ Haus mit einem schön___
    Garten in einer klein___ Stadt.   — -en, -en, -en
94. Hier ist die Adresse des deutsch___ Arztes, der deutsch___
    Apotheke und des neu___ Krankenhauses.   — -en, -en, -en
95. Würden Sie bitte diesen amerikanisch___ Touristen helfen,
    ihre schwer___ Koffer auf die richtig___ Zimmer zu bringen?   — -en, -en, -en
96. Fragen Sie den jung___ Mann dort!   — -en
97. Ich gebe immer ein gut___ Trinkgeld.   — -es
98. Haben Sie noch ein Zimmer frei___?   — no ending

Probe-Test

A. *Translate the underlined expressions.*

1. Manche Leute <u>werden immer</u> „ein Haar in der Suppe" <u>finden</u>. _____

2. <u>Wenn man nichts weiß</u>, soll man den Mund halten. _____

3. Benzin <u>wird</u> nicht immer billig <u>sein</u>. _____

4. <u>Wann nimmt man</u> sich etwas zu Herzen? _____

5. <u>Werden Sie ihm glauben?</u> _____

B. *Express in German.*

1. When will he come? _____

2. We will call you if we have time. _____

3. I hope I won't get sick. _____

4. I don't want to come. _____

5. When I was in Germany, it was not so expensive. _____

   _____

6. If you write me, I shall answer you. _____

7. I will buy it tomorrow. _____

C. *Answer as appropriate.*

1. The future tense in German is formed with _____.

   _____.

2. In a main clause in the future tense, the _____ stands at the end of the clause.

3. When a modal is used in the future tense, the _____

   stands at the end.

D. *Create sentences by arranging the cue words in their proper sequence.*

1. (werden/solche Redensarten/Sie/oft/hören)

   _____

2. (solche Redensarten/oft/hören/ich/werde)

   Ich weiß daß, _____

3. (Sie/solche Redensarten/oft/in Deutschland/müssen/hören/werden)

   _____

   _____

E. *Complete with the appropriate form of the descriptive adjective.*

1. Ich möchte diese junge Katze kaufen. Ich möchte eine _____ Katze kaufen.

2. Was kostet ein junger Kater? Was kostet dieser _____ Kater?

3. Wann bringst du uns das kleine Kätzchen? Wann bringst du uns ein _____ Kätzchen?

4. Warum kaufst du nicht diesen deutschen Schäferhund? Warum kaufst du nicht einen

   _____ Schäferhund?

5. Wem gibst du deine junge Katze? Wem gibst du eine _____ Katze?

6. Wo kann ich das schöne Tier kaufen? Wo kann ich ein _____ Tier kaufen?

7. Das ist der Regenmantel der jungen Amerikanerin. Das ist der Regenmantel einer

_____ Amerikanerin.

8. Das Auto gehört einem guten Kunden. Das Auto gehört diesem _____ Kunden.

F. *Complete with the correct form of the cue adjective.*

1. (kalt)   Bringen Sie mir bitte ein _____ Bier!

2. (heiß)   Bringen Sie mir bitte einen _____ Kaffee!

3. (schwer)   Ist das ein _____ Fehler?

4. (jung)   Wer ist der _____ Student dort?

5. (deutsch)   Er wohnt bei einer _____ Familie.

G. *Supply* **als,** **wenn,** *or* **wann.**

1. _____ sagt man, „ich habe die Nase voll"?

2. _____ ich in Deutschland war, hörte ich viele Redensarten.

3. Er schimpft mich immer, _____ ich nicht den Mund halte.

4. Man hält den Daumen, _____ man jemand Glück wünscht.

H. *Cross out the incorrect word in the idiom and replace it with the right one.*

1. Ich werde dir den Fuß waschen.

2. Deutsch ist mir ein Dorn im Ohr.

3. Die Universität hängt mir zum Mund 'raus.

I. *Cross out the word that does not belong in the sentence.*

1. Was er erzählt, hat weder oder Hand noch Fuß.

2. Sie müssen immer nie ein Haar in der Suppe finden.

3. Er hat ein kurzes langes Gesicht gemacht.

J. *Complete with the appropriate word from the list.*

Bart   Ohren   Finger   Nase   Daumen
Mund   Schulter   Kopf   Augen

1. Mit den _____ sieht man.

2. Mit den _____ hört man.

3. Die _____ und der _____ sind an der Hand.

4. Der _____ und die _____ sind im Gesicht.

5. Mit dem _____ spricht man.

K. *Somebody tells you the following. Write a response.*

1. Warum soll ich das auf die leichte Schulter nehmen? _____

   _____

2. Sie haben mich mit diesem schlechten Auto übers Ohr gehauen. _____

   _____

3. Du gehst mir auf die Nerven! _____

   _____

L. *Complete with the German equivalent of the cue.*

1. (*neither . . . nor*) Das hat _____ Hand _____ Fuß.

2. (*good luck*) Ich wünsche dir viel _____.

3. (*to*) Von Kopf _____ Fuß, von oben _____ unten.

4. (*ads*) Es gibt zu viele _____.

5. (*matter*) Ich habe genug von dieser _____.

M. *Circle the idiomatic German equivalent of the underlined English word.*

1. *He has a <u>hangover</u>.* Er hat (einen Kater/eine Katze).

2. *This is a thorn in my side.* Dies ist mir ein Dorn (in der Seite/im Auge).

N. *Explain to a German student learning English the meaning of:*

1. *"You are pulling my leg."*
Das bedeutet: _____

_____

2. *"He put his foot in his mouth."*
Das bedeutet: _____

_____

3. *"I am crossing my fingers for you."*
Das bedeutet: _____

_____

Erweitern Sie Ihren Wortschatz!

A. Englisch-Deutsch

1. good luck _____

2. factory _____

3. part _____

4. life _____

5. hair _____

6. ear _____

7. cat _____

8. eye _____

9. face _____

10. to watch television _____

11. to wash _____

12. to criticize _____

13. to wish _____

14. to feel well _____

15. to press _____

16. disappointed _____

17. dirty _____

18. pessimistic _____

19. yesterday _____

20. quiet _____

    _____

21. to shut up _____

22. to cross your fingers for someone _____

    _____

23. to look disappointed _____

24. to make a long face _____

25. to go to the dogs _____

B. Deutsch-Englisch

1. das Wettrüsten _____

2. das Jahrhundert _____

3. das Tier _____

4. die Qualität _____

5. der Kater _____

6. der Mund _____

7. das Toilettenpapier _____

8. das Waschmittel _____

9. profitieren _____

10. schimpfen _____

11. erleben _____

12. nachdenken _____

13. fühlen _____

14. ausgeben _____

15. lebendig _____

16. einzeln _____

17. menschlich _____

18. ernst _____

19. jemand _____

20. zum Hals heraushängen _____

21. auf den Arm nehmen _____

22. die Nase voll haben _____

23. jemand übers Ohr hauen _____

_____

24. etwas hat weder Hand noch Fuß _____

_____

25. etwas auf die leichte Schulter nehmen _____

_____

Hör zu . . .und antworte!   Antwortbogen

Übung **A**.   *Circle* **Logisch** *or* **Unlogisch**.

1. A   B   2. A   B   3. A   B   4. A   B   5. A   B   6. A   B

Übung **B**.   **Diktat**.

1. _____

2. _____

3. _____

Übung **C**.   *Write down the correct word.*

1. _____   2. _____   3. _____   4. _____

5. _____   6. _____   7. _____   8. _____

9. _____   10. _____   11. _____

Übung **D**.   *Circle A, B, or* **Richtig**.

1. A   B   R   2. A   B   R   3. A   B   R   4. A   B   R

5. A   B   R   6. A   B   R   7. A   B   R   8. A   B   R

9. A   B   R   10. A   B   R   11. A   B   R   12. A   B   R

13. A   B   R

Kapitel 11

Selbst-Test

DIALOG

Translate the underlined expressions.

1. Hauptmann <u>wurde</u> schnell <u>berühmt</u>.
2. <u>War das dein Ernst?</u>
3. <u>Für was müssen Sie mich halten?</u>

4. Beide <u>werden rot</u>.
5. <u>Fühlen Sie mal!</u>

— became famous
— Were you serious?
— What must you think of me?

— blush
— Go ahead, feel (it).

1. The der-words and ein-words (continuation)

6. The seven most common **der**-words are: _____, _____,
   _____, _____, _____, _____, and _____.

— **dies-, jed-, jen-, manch-, solch-, welch-, all-**

7. The **ein**-words are **ein** and **kein** plus the possessive adjectives: _____, _____, _____, _____, _____, _____,
   _____, _____.

— **mein, dein, sein, ihr, unser, euer, ihr, Ihr**

8. These words are called **der**-words and **ein**-words because they follow the declension pattern of _____ and _____.

— **der, ein**

9. The **der**-words and **ein**-words are (descriptive/limiting) adjectives.

— limiting

*Replace the underlined definite or indefinite article by the cue **der**-word or **ein**-word.*

10. (dies-) Kennst du <u>eine</u> Geschichte von Homer? _____

— diese

11. (all-) Heinrich las <u>die</u> Geschichten <u>der</u> alten Römer.
    _____, _____

— alle, aller

12. (welch-) In <u>dem</u> Geschäft arbeitet er? _____

— welchem

13. (unser-)   Sie können in <u>einem</u> großen Geschäft viel Geld
    verdienen. _____   — uns(e)rem
14. (sein-)   Er gründete <u>eine</u> eigene Firma. _____   — seine
15. (jed-)   Er suchte Troja unter <u>dem</u> Hügel. _____   — jedem
16. (Manch-)   <u>Der</u> Wissenschaftler glaubte ihm nicht. _____ — Mancher
17. (solch-)   Wem gehörten <u>die</u> wunderbaren Schätze? _____ — solche
18. (kein-)   Schliemann zeigte <u>dem</u> Arbeiter das Gold. _____ — keinem
19. (ihr-)   Flohen die Trojaner nicht aus <u>einer</u> brennenden
    Stadt? _____   — ihrer

2. Adjectives preceded by **der**-words and **ein**-words (Continuation)

20.. The ending of a descriptive adjective depends on whether
    the adjective is preceded by a _____ or an _____.   — **der**-word, **ein**-word
21. A choice between endings has to be made only in three
    instances: 1) _____ _____ _____, 2) _____ _____ _____,   — masculine nomina-
    3) _____ _____ _____.   tive singular; neuter
                                                                   nominative singular;
                                                                   neuter accusative
                                                                   singular

*Restate, substituting the cue determiner and adjusting the adjective
ending if necessary.*

22. (unser-)   Die Bevölkerungsexplosion ist zu dem großen
    Problem geworden. Die Bevölkerungsexplosion ist zu _____
    _____ Problem geworden.   — unserem großen
23. (jen-)   Wann erreichen wir einen kritischen Punkt in dieser
    Explosion? Wann erreichen wir _____ _____ Punkt in
    dieser Explosion?   — jenen kritischen
24. (Manch-)   Ihr kleines Land hat eine zu große Bevölkerung.
    _____ _____ Land hat eine zu große Bevölkerung.   — Manches kleine (*or*
                                                                   Manch kleines)
25. (Welch-?)   Ein europäisches Land hat keine Bevölkerungs-
    explosion. _____ _____ Land hat keine Bevölkerungs-
    explosion?   — Welches europäische
                                                                   (*or* Welch
                                                                   europäisches)

26. (jed-)   Die Bevölkerungsexplosion ist für euer armes Land
    ein Problem. Die Bevölkerungsexplosion ist für _____
    _____ Land ein Problem.   — jedes arme

Supply the appropriate ending.

27. Hast du diesen interessant_____ Artikel gelesen?   — -en
28. Der Artikel spricht von unserer groß_____ Bevölkerungs-
    explosion.   — -en

29. Weißt du, daß ein jung____ Ehepaar heute nur zwei Kinder
    haben soll?   — -es

30. Ja sicher, aber manches jung____ Ehepaar wird dagegen
    protestieren.   — -e

31. Dein jung____ Bruder und seine nett____ Frau wollen auch
    kein____ Kinder.   — -er, -e, -e

32. Schön, aber wir wollen doch ein lieb____, klein____ Baby,
    nicht wahr?   — -es, -es

3. Unpreceded adjectives

33. When no limiting adjective precedes the descriptive
    adjective, the descriptive adjective adds the appropriate
    _____ ending.   — primary

34. Except for two instances, the primary ending is the same
    as the ending of the (definite article/limiting adjective/
    definite article or limiting adjective).   — definite article or
                                                           limiting adjective

35. The two instances where the endings differ are the singular
    masculine and neuter singular _____ case.   — genitive

36. In these cases, the ending is _____ instead of _____.   — **-en, -es**

*Restate without the limiting adjective. Make any necessary changes
in the unpreceded adjective.*

37. Dieser gute Wein ist teuer. _____ Wein ist teuer.   — Guter

38. Diese kalte Milch schmeckt gut. _____ Milch schmeckt gut. — Kalte

39. Ein deutsches Mädchen sucht Arbeit. _____ Mädchen
    sucht Arbeit.   — Deutsches

40. Es macht uns einen großen Spaß. Es macht uns _____
    Spaß.   — großen

41. Möchten Sie eine warme Milch? Möchten Sie _____
    Milch?   — warme

42. Kaufen Sie immer dieses kalifornische Obst? Kaufen Sie
    immer _____ Obst?   — kalifornisches

43. Wer ist der Junge mit dem schwarzen Haar? Wer ist der
    Junge mit _____ Haar?   — schwarzem

44. Er handelt nach einer alten Tradition. Er handelt nach
    _____ Tradition.   — alter

45. Bei diesem kalten Wetter bleibe ich zu Haus. Bei _____
    Wetter bleibe ich zu Haus.   — kaltem

46. Ich liebe das Aroma dieses echten Kaffees. Ich liebe das
    Aroma _____ Kaffees.   — echten

47. Das ist das Resultat einer guten Arbeit. Das ist das Resultat
    _____ Arbeit.   — guter

48. Was ist der Wert dieses japanischen Geldes? Was ist der
    Wert _____ Geldes?   — japanischen

49. Diese alten Klischees gefallen mir nicht. _____ Klischees gefallen mir nicht.

    — Alte

50. Er hat keine großen Entdeckungen gemacht. Er hat _____ Entdeckungen gemacht.

    — große

51. Wir sprechen von dem Recht der amerikanischen Frauen. Wir sprechen von dem Recht _____ Frauen.

    — amerikanischer

52. Das ist die Meinung mancher jungen Leute. Das ist die Meinung _____ Leute.

    — junger

4. Participles used as adjectives

53. Past and _____ participles can be used as adjectives.

    — present

54. The present participle is formed by adding _____ to the _____.

    — **-d**, infinitive

55. When used as adjectives, both past and present participles use endings that are (the same as/different from) those of regular adjectives.

    — the same as

Turn the cue verb into a past participle and use it as an adjective.

brauchen   *to use*

56. Ich habe einen _____ Volkswagen zu verkaufen.

    — gebrauchten

57. _____ Volkswagen zu verkaufen!

    — Gebrauchter

58. _____ Auto zu verkaufen!

    — Gebrauchtes

entlaufen   *to run away*

59. Wer hat unseren _____ Hund gesehen?

    — entlaufenen

60. _____ Schäferhund gefunden!

    — Entlaufener

61. Wem gehört diese _____ Katze?

    — entlaufene

Turn the cue verb into a present participle and use it as an adjective.

brennen   *to burn*

62. Das ist ein _____ Problem.

    — brennendes

63. Von welchem _____ Problem sprechen Sie?

    — brennenden

64. Dieses _____ Problem müssen Sie verstehen.

    — brennende

bellen   *to bark*

65. _____ Hunde beißen nicht.

    — Bellende

66. Dieser _____ Hund geht mir auf die Nerven.

    — bellende

67. Ein _____ Hund ist auch gefährlich.

    — bellender

5. Adjectives and participles used as nouns

68. When an adjective or participle is used as a noun, it is spelled with a _____ letter.

    — capital

Form nouns from the cue adjectives and participles.

69. **reisend** *a traveler* (male) _____ _____   — ein Reisender
70. **reisend** *a traveler* (female) _____ _____   — eine Reisende

    krank
71. *a sick person* (male) _____ _____   — ein Kranker
72. *the sick person* (female) _____ _____   — die Kranke

    erwachsen
73. *the grown up person, adult* (male) _____ _____   — der Erwachsene
74. *an adult* (female) _____ _____   — eine Erwachsene

    geliebt
75. *my lover* (male) _____ _____   — mein Geliebter
76. *to my lover* (female) _____ _____   — meiner Geliebten

    verlassen
77. *the abandoned person* (female) _____ _____   — die Verlassene
78. *from an abandoned one* (male) _____ _____ _____   — von einem Verlassenen

6. Ordinal numbers

79. Ordinal numbers show the rank of something in a _____.   — series
80. The _____ article is always used with ordinal numbers.   — definite
81. Through 19, ordinal numbers are formed by adding _____ to the cardinal number; from 20 on, they add _____.   — -t-, -st-
82. Ordinal numbers (are/are not) declined like adjectives.   — are

Complete with German equivalent of the cue ordinal number.

83. (*first*) Ja, Fritzchen ist unser _____ Kind.   — erstes
84. (*first*) Sind Sie zum _____ Mal in Deutschland?   — ersten
85. (*third*) Ich habe noch eine _____ Frage.   — dritte
86. (*seventh*) Sie sind im _____ Himmel!   — siebten (*or* siebenten)
87. (*eighth*) Wir wohnen im _____ Stock.   — achten
88. (*nineteenth*) Welcher Tag ist der _____ März?   — neunzehnte
89. (*twentieth*) Morgen ist der _____ des Monats.   — zwanzigste
90. (*thirty-first*) Ja, sie ist am _____ Mai geboren.   — einunddreißigsten
91. (*fiftieth*) Hawaii ist der _____ Staat.   — fünfzigste
92. (*hundredth*) Ich habe dir das schon zum _____ Mal gesagt!   — hundertsten
93. (*twenty-ninth*) Alle vier Jahre gibt es einen _____ Februar.   — neunundzwanzigsten

94. (*twenty-first*) Er besucht uns zu meinem _____ Geburtstag. — einundzwanzigsten

95. (*sixteenth*) Nach dem _____ Mai komme ich wieder. — sechzehnten

96. (*thirty-first*) Der _____ Dezember ist der letzte Tag des Jahres. — einunddreißigste

97. From **Drittel** on, German fractions are formed by adding _____ to the ordinal number. — -l

Complete with the cue fraction.

98. $\left(\frac{1}{4}\right)$ Ich möchte ein _____ Pfund Kaffee. — viertel

99. $\left(\frac{2}{3}\right)$ _____ der Bevölkerung arbeitet. — Zwei Drittel

100. $\left(\frac{3}{4}\right)$ Es ist _____ Kilo zu schwer. — dreiviertel

101. The German word for *half* is _____ or **die** _____. — **halb, Hälfte**

102. **Halb** (is/is not) declined. — is

Complete with **halb-**.

103. Er war ein _____ Jahr krank. — halbes

104. Wir warten schon eine _____ Stunde. — halbe

105. Der Zug fährt in einer _____ Stunde. — halben

106. Ordinal adverbs are used for (ranking/emphasis). — ranking

Complete with the German equivalent.

107. (*Firstly*) _____ habe ich keine Zeit, und (*secondly*) _____ habe ich kein Geld. — Erstens, zweitens

Probe-Test

A. *Translate the underlined expressions.*

1. Wie einfach haben es doch <u>englischsprechende Menschen</u>! _____

    _____

2. Wann duzen sich <u>Erwachsene</u>? _____

3. <u>Wenn man gute Freunde wird.</u> _____

    _____

4. <u>Wollen wir</u> ein Volk von Duzern <u>werden</u>? _____

B. 1. The **der**-words and **ein**-words follow the declensional pattern of the _____

    and _____ articles.

2. The **ein**-words are all the _____ adjectives.

3. Cross out the word that is not a **der**-word: **dies-, jed-, manch-, solch-, viel-, welch-, all-.**

4. **Der**-words and **ein**-words are (limiting/descriptive) adjectives. _____

C. *Complete the sentence with the cue **der**-word or **ein**-word.*

1. (Welch-) _____ Regel meinen Sie?

2. (Welch-) _____ Beispiel verwendet er?

3. (Welch-) _____ Fehler habe ich gemacht?

4. (all-) Man sagt nicht zu _____ Menschen „du".

5. (Manch-) _____ Leute machen diesen Fehler.

6. (jed-) Man spricht mit _____ Kind per „du".

7. (ihr) Sie sagt immer „du" zu _____ Schülern.

8. (sein) Natürlich sagt er „du" zu _____ Frau.

9. (unser) Der Lehrer hat zu _____ Kind „Du Rindvieh" gesagt!

10. (Mein) _____ Freundin sagt jetzt „du" zu mir.

11. (mein) Kennst du _____ Freund?

D. *Complete with the appropriate form of the cue adjective.*

1. (neu) Heute kostet jedes _____ Auto viel Geld.

2. (neu) Was hat dein _____ Auto gekostet?

3. (neu) Von welchem _____ Auto sprechen Sie?

4. (neu) Die Farbe deines _____ Autos gefällt mir gut.

5. (jung) Dieser _____ Mann möchte Sie sprechen.

6. (jung) Sie hat mit jedem _____ Mann getanzt.

7. (jung) Kennst du keinen _____ Mann dort?

8. (jung) Ja, das ist ihr _____ Mann.

9. (deutsch) Ist das deine _____ Freundin?

10. (deutsch) Erzähl' uns von deiner _____ Freundin!

11. (deutsch) Das Auto gehört meiner _____ Freundin.

12. (deutsch) Mit welcher _____ Freundin kommt er?

13. (arm) Er hilft allen _____ Leuten.

14. (arm) Manche _____ Leute sind gar nicht so arm wie es scheint.

15. (arm) Kennst du denn keine _____ Leute?

16. (arm) Das Leben dieser _____ Leute ist schwer.

E. *Complete with the proper form of the descriptive adjective.*

1. (reich) Er ist das Kind _____ Leute.

2. (reich) Er ist das Kind von _____ Leuten.

3. (reich) Er ist das Kind dieser _____ Leute.

4. (gut) Ein _____ Wein ist teuer.

5. (gut) _____ Wein ist teuer.

6. (gut) Welchen _____ Wein trinken Sie heute?

7. (schön) Hier ist immer _____ Wetter.

8. (schön) Bei _____ Wetter gehen wir in die Berge.

9. (schön) Trotz des _____ Wetters war es kalt.

10. (alt) Das ist so Sitte nach _____ Tradition.

11. (alt) Nach einer _____ Tradition feiert man dieses Ereignis mit einem Glas Wein.

12. (alt) Das ist _____ Tradition bei uns.

F. *Rewrite the sentence, omitting the* **der**-*word or* **ein**-*word.*

1. Dieses frische Obst ist gut. _____ Obst ist gut.

2. Dieses eiskalte Bier ist ungesund. _____ Bier ist ungesund.

3. Bei diesem schlechten Wetter bleiben wir zu Haus. Bei _____ Wetter bleiben wir zu Haus.

4. Er trinkt kein eiskaltes Bier. Er trinkt _____ Bier.

5. Sie ißt gern Wienerschnitzel mit einem grünen Salat. Sie ißt gern Wienerschnitzel mit

_____ Salat.

G. *Complete with the past participle or present participle of the cue infinitive and use it as an adjective with the appropriate ending.*

1. (feiern)   Das ist ein oft _____ Ereignis.

2. (erwachsen)   Was sagt man zu einem _____ Mädchen?

3. (lächeln)   Wer ist das _____ Mädchen dort?

4. (sterben)   Sind die Deutschen ein _____ Volk?

H. 1. Adjectives and participles can also be used as _____.

I. *Rewrite, replacing the underlined words with a noun.*

1. Dem kranken Jungen geht es besser. _____

_____

2. Kennst du die deutsche Dame dort? _____

_____

3. Sie helfen den angekommenen Kindern. _____

_____

4. Das ist die Meinung eines erwachsenen Menschen. _____

_____

J. *Complete the statement by writing out the cue ordinal number.*

1. (16) Man sagt „du'' bis zum _____ Lebensjahr.

2. (1) Das ist mein _____ Fehler.

3. (100) Ich sage es dir zum _____ Mal!

4. (3) Wir wohnen im _____ Stock.

5. (7) Heute ist der _____ Tag der Woche.

6. (12) Dezember ist der _____ Monat.

7. (1, 2) Er war im _____ und _____ Weltkrieg.

8. (24) Weihnachten ist am _____ Dezember.

K. *Write out the date in numerals as you would in German.*

1. March 2, 1985 _____

2. December 27, 1986 _____

L. *Write out the date as you would in German, spelling out the month but using the number for the day.*

1. (6.7.) Heute ist der _____ 1986.

2. (9.3.) Heute ist der _____ 1986.

3. (7.5.) Berlin, den _____ 1986.

M. *Express in German.*

1. Every family knows these problems.

   _____

2. His father works for a German firm.

   _____

3. German wine tastes good.

_____

4. He read her long letters every day.

_____

5. Which German girl did he marry?

_____

6. She did not make any mistakes in this long test.

_____

7. Her new car didn't cost too much.

_____

8. This is my third year in a German-speaking country.

_____

N. *Complete the two-paragraph passage below with the correct form of the German adjective. (The adjectives are grouped by paragraph.)*

    (1) deutsche/deutschen

        ersten/erstes

        großer/großen

        junge/junger

        leidende/leidender

        naturalistischen/naturalistischem

        protestierender/protestierenden

        schwerem/schweren

        vieldiskutiertes/vieldiskutierten

        vollen/vollem

    (2) alte/alter

        bahnbrechendem/bahnbrechenden

        egoistischer/egoistischen

        gesunde/gesunden

        großer/großen

        herzloser/herzlose

        hübsche/hübscher

        junge/junger

        nächste/nächsten

        schöne/schönen

        schreckliches/schreckliche

        stille/stillen

        typisch/typisches

        unglückliche/unglückliches

        unmenschlicher/unmenschlichen

        verheiratete/verheirateten

        wichtige/wichtiger

(1) Der _____ Dichter Gerhart Hauptmann wurde mit seinem
     young

_____ Drama weltberühmt. In diesem
   naturalistic

_____ Stück zeigte man zum _____
   much debated   *first*

Mal die Geburt eines Kindes auf einer _____ Bühne. „Vor Sonnenaufgang"
                 German

führte zu einem _____ Theaterskandal. Als die _____
       big   *suffering*

Mutter bei der _____ Geburt nach dem Arzt ruft, warf ein
      difficult

_____ Theaterbesucher eine Geburtszange[1] aus dem
   protesting

_____ Theatersaal[2] auf die Bühne.
  full

(2) In diesem _____ Stück trifft ein _____ Idealist—
        pioneering   *young*

er heißt Alfred Loth—die _____ Helene Krause. Der
         pretty

_____ Schritt vom „Sie" zum „du" geschieht[3] in einer _____
  important   *quiet*

Laube. Als Loth jedoch am _____ Tag herausfindet[4], daß die
          next

_____ Schwester von Helene und ihr _____ Vater
   married   *old*

[1] *forceps* [2] **der Saal** *hall* [3] *takes place* [4] *finds out*

Alkoholiker sind, verläßt der _____ Loth die
heartless

_____ Helene. Loth fürchtet, daß er von Helene keine
unhappy

_____ Kinder bekommen wird. Loth ist ein Idealist—aber ein
healthy

_____ Idealist. Seine _____ Ideale haben für
egotistic   *beautiful*

ihn mehr Wert als Helene. Helene kann ihren _____
inhuman

Verlobten nicht verstehen. Sie nimmt sich das Leben . . . sie tötet sich mit einem

_____ Messer. ,,Vor Sonnenaufgang'' ist ein _____
big   *typical*

Drama des Naturalismus. Es zeigt uns keine _____, sondern eine
pretty

_____ Welt. Eine Welt wie sie in Wirklichkeit[1] ist.
horrible

O. Reading comprehension

Explain in a few words in English why Germans would get a kick out of this joke—and you, too, now that you have been introduced to the intricacies of the use of **Sie** *and* **du**.

Der kleine Emil war in der Schule nicht brav. Er hat zum Lehrer ,,du'' gesagt. Er
muß zur Strafe (*punishment*) hundertmal schreiben: ,,Ich darf den Lehrer
nicht duzen.'' Emil schreibt den Satz zweihundertmal. ,,Warum hast du das
zweihundertmal geschrieben?'' fragt der Lehrer. Emil antwortet: ,,Ich wollte
dich glücklich machen.''

Germans would enjoy this joke because _____

_____

[1] *in reality*

Erweitern Sie Ihren Wortschatz!

A. Englisch-Deutsch

1. teacher (female) _____

2. kiss _____

3. reader _____

4. knee _____

5. step _____

6. scandal _____

7. sunrise _____

8. way _____

9. glass _____

10. theater _____

11. to address with **du** _____

12. to untie _____

13. to throw _____

14. to kiss _____

15. to sit down _____

16. to lose _____

17. to give back _____

18. somebody _____

19. offended _____

20. loud(ly) _____

21. short _____

22. unnatural _____

23. a short time ago _____

24. to be on a "du" basis _____

_____

25. to blush _____

B. Deutsch-Englisch

1. die Bühne _____

2. das Ereignis _____

3. die Regel _____

4. die Änderung _____

5. das Schweigen _____

6. der Lieblingsplatz _____

7. der Erwachsene _____

8. das erste Mal _____

9. die Seide _____

10. der Ausschnitt _____

11. entscheiden _____

12. sich schämen _____

13. bahnen _____

14. siezen _____

15. losmachen _____

16. vorhin _____

17. schrecklich _____

18. jedoch _____

19. ungestört _____

20. komisch _____

21. hübsch _____

22. die meisten _____

23. War das nicht dein Ernst? _____

_____

24. Für was müssen Sie mich halten? _____

_____

25. sich jemand an den Hals werfen _____

_____

Hör zu . . .und antworte!   Antwortbogen

Übung **A.**   *Circle A or B.*

1. A   B   2. A   B   3. A   B   4. A   B   5. A   B   6. A   B

Übung **B.**   *Circle the word you hear.*

1. Tasse   Tatze   Katze   2. Schweiß   Schweiz   Mais   3. Tal   Zahl   Saal

4. Malz   Pfalz   Salz   5. so   Zoo   Zoll   6. lahm   Lamm   Schlamm

7. Schacht   scharrt   lacht   8. Bart   Art   Fahrt   9. schön   schon   Föhn

10. Söhne   Sehne   Lehne

Übung **C.**   *Circle A, B, or C.*

1. A   B   C   2. A   B   C   3. A   B   C   4. A   B   C

5. A   B   C   6. A   B   C   7. A   B   C   8. A   B   C

9. A   B   C   10. A   B   C   11. A   B   C   12. A   B   C

Übung **D**. *Write down the correct number or answer.*

1. _____ 2. _____ 3. _____ 4. _____

5. _____ 6. _____ 7. _____ 8. _____

9. _____ 10. _____ 11. _____ 12. _____

Kapitel 12

Selbst-Test

DIALOG

Translate the underlined expressions.

1. <u>Du bekommst davon die weißesten Zähne.</u>
    — This will give you the whitest teeth.

2. Jedes Jahr <u>werden sie schlimmer.</u>
    — they become worse
3. <u>Das stimmt nicht.</u>
    — That is not correct.
4. Wir <u>lassen uns</u> von der Reklame <u>manipulieren.</u>
    — We let ourselves be manipulated
5. <u>Daran läßt sich nichts ändern.</u>
    — Nothing can be done about it

1. The comparison of adjectives and adverbs

6. The three forms of adjectives and adverbs are: the positive, the _____, and the _____.
    — comparative, superlative

7. The comparative is formed by adding _____ to the stem of the adjective or adverb.
    — -er
8. One-syllable adjectives and adverbs usually add an _____ to the stem vowel.
    — umlaut

Give the comparative forms.

9. schnell _____, groß _____
    — schneller, größer
10. schön _____, alt _____
    — schöner, älter
11. jung _____, oft _____
    — jünger, öfter
12. alt _____, weiß _____
    — älter, weißer

13. In English, the comparative of words of more than one syllable is often formed with the help of the word _____.
    — *more*

14. In German, the word **mehr** (is/is not) used to form the comparative with adjectives and adverbs.
— is not

Complete.

15. *This brand is cheaper.* Diese Marke ist _____.
— billiger
16. *This brand is more expensive.* Diese Marke ist _____.
— teurer
17. *This brand costs more.* Diese Marke _____ _____.
— kostet mehr

18. The German superlative is formed by adding _____ to the stem.
— -st
19. One-syllable adjectives (usually/rarely) add an umlaut in the superlative form.
— usually
20. A linking **-e-** is usually inserted between the stem and the **-st** ending when the stem ends in a _____ sound or in the letter _____ or _____.
— "hissing", **-d**, **-t**
21. When an adjective in the comparative or superlative precedes the noun it modifies, it (adds/does not add) the same endings as any other adjective.
— adds

Give the superlative forms without any adjectival ending.

22. klein _____, lang _____
— kleinst-, längst-
23. gesund _____, weiß _____
— gesündest-, weißest-

Complete with the correct ending.

24. Kennen Sie meinen jünger____ Bruder?
— -en
25. Das ist der jünger____ Bruder von den beiden.
— -e
26. Wie heißt dein jünger____ Bruder?
— -er
27. Wir sprechen von Ihrem jünger____ Bruder.
— -en
28. Das Auto gehört meiner ältest____ Schwester.
— -en
29. Dies ist meine ältest____ Schwester.
— -e
30. Wie heißt Ihr jüngst____ Kind?
— -es
31. Das jüngst____ Kind heißt Brenda.
— -e

Give the positive, comparative, and superlative forms.

32. *gladly* _____ _____ _____
— gern, lieber, liebst-
33. *good* _____ _____ _____
— gut, besser, best-
34. *much* _____ _____ _____
— viel, mehr, meist-
35. *high* _____ _____ _____
— hoch, höher, höchst-

36. The **am** superlative is used with adjectives not preceded by the _____ article and with all _____.
— definite, adverbs
37. Similarity is expressed by the _____ form of the adjective or adverb with _____ *as . . . as.*
— positive, **so . . . wie**
38. Dissimilarity is expressed by the _____ with _____ *as, then.*
— comparative, **als**

Complete as suggested by the cue.

39. (*as expensive as*) Silber ist nicht _____ Gold. — so teuer wie
40. (*as big as*) Die BRD ist _____ Oregon. — so groß wie
41. (*higher than*) Ein Jet fliegt _____ ein Propellerflugzeug. — höher als
42. (*less than*) Ein Ford kostet _____ ein Cadillac. — weniger als

Complete with the comparative and superlative forms.

43. Fritz ist intelligent, Moritz ist _____, aber Marlene ist _____. — intelligenter, am intelligentesten

44. Dieser Jet fliegt schnell, die Concorde fliegt _____, aber
    Superman fliegt _____! — schneller, am schnellsten

45. Wilhelm hat einen langen Bart, Fritz hat einen _____
    Bart, aber der Weihnachtsmann hat den _____. — längeren, längsten

46. German expresses an increase in degree with _____ plus
    the comparative. — immer

47. A relationship between two comparatives is expressed in
    German by the construction _____ *the . . . the.* — je . . . desto

48. In this construction, **desto** is often replaced by either
    _____ or _____. — je, umso

49. Do not confuse the **-er** ending of the comparative with the
    _____ ending **-er**. — adjectival

*Complete with the appropriate form of the cue adjective, and give
the English equivalent.*

50. (*klein*) Das ist mein _____ Bruder. — kleiner *small*
51. (*klein*) Je _____ desto besser. — kleiner *smaller*
52. (*schnell*) Ein Porsche ist ein _____ Auto. — schnelles *fast*
53. (*schnell*) Dieser hier ist noch _____. — schneller *faster*

Complete with the German equivalent of the English cues.

54. (*colder and colder*) Es wird _____. — immer kälter
55. (*like best*) Ich habe es _____. — am liebsten
56. (*bigger than*) Robert ist _____ Erich. — größer als
57. (*cheaper*) Das ist der _____ Regenschirm. — billigere
58. (*most beautiful*) Hier ist unser _____ Zimmer. — schönstes
59. (*most expensive*) Hier ist der _____ Koffer. — teuerste
60. (*the most expensive*) Welcher Koffer ist _____? — am teuersten

2. The construction **um . . . zu** + infinitive

61. The construction **um . . . zu** plus the infinitive always corre-
    sponds to English _____ plus the infinitive. — *in order to*

Complete the German equivalent.

62. *I eat in order to live and do not live in order to eat.* Ich esse,
    _____ und lebe nicht, _____.

— um zu leben, um zu essen

63. *The company advertises in order to sell more toothpaste.* Die
    Firma macht Reklame, _____.

— um mehr Zahnpaste zu verkaufen

3. Nouns after **etwas, nichts, viel, wenig**

64. Adjectives after **etwas, nichts, viel,** and **wenig** are treated
    like _____ and always end in _____.

— nouns, **-es**

Complete with the German equivalent of the English cue.

65. (*something new*) Wissen Sie _____ _____?
66. (*nothing interesting*) Es gab _____ _____ zu sehen.
67. (*much good*) Sie hat _____ _____ in ihrem Leben getan.
68. (*little good*) Er hat _____ _____ zu erzählen.

— etwas Neues
— nichts Interessantes
— viel Gutes
— wenig Gutes

4. **lassen** and **sich lassen**

69. The three basic meanings of **lassen** are: *to* _____; *to* _____;
    and *to* _____ *someone to do something.*

— *leave; let* (or *permit*); *cause*

Translate the underlined constructions.

70. <u>Lassen</u> Sie mich bitte nicht lange <u>warten</u>!
71. <u>Lassen</u> Sie mich allein!
72. Er <u>läßt</u> immer sein Auto hier.
73. Sie <u>hat</u> ihr Auto <u>reparieren lassen</u>.
74. Wo <u>haben</u> Sie Ihren Regenschirm <u>gelassen</u>?
75. Ich <u>lasse</u> dich <u>tun</u>, was du willst.

— *let . . . wait*
— *Leave me alone!*
— *leaves*
— *had . . . repaired*
— *did . . . leave*
— *let . . . do*

5. Possessive pronouns

76. Possessive adjectives become possessive pronouns when they (are used with/replace) a noun.

    — replace

77. When they are used as pronouns, the possessives take the same endings as _____-words.

    — **der**

Complete with the correct form of the possessive pronoun.

78. Ich habe meinen Koffer. Hast du _____?

    — deinen

79. Er hat sein Geld bekommen, aber ich habe _____ noch nicht bekommen.

    — meines (*or* meins)

80. Mein Auto ist kaputt. Wir müssen mit _____ fahren, Frau Schulz.

    — Ihrem

81. Das Haus gehört nicht euren Eltern, sondern _____ (*ours*).

    — unseren (*or* unsren)

82. Kennst du Fritz und Inge? Fritz ist nicht mein Bruder, sondern _____.

    — ihrer

83. Kennst du Vicky und Rudolf? Die kleine Berta ist nicht ihr Kind, sondern _____.

    — seins (*or* seines)

84. The indefinite article **ein** and its negative **kein** can (also/never) be used as pronouns.

    — also

Complete with the proper form of **ein** *or* **kein.**

85. Hast du einen Regenschirm? Ich habe leider _____.

    — keinen

86. Er hat ein Auto und ich habe auch _____.

    — eins (*or* eines)

87. Ich helfe diesem Kind. Willst du auch _____ helfen?

    — einem

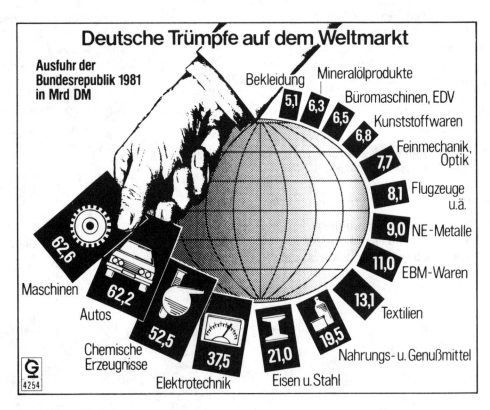

Deutsche Trümpfe auf dem Weltmarkt

Ausfuhr der
Bundesrepublik 1981
in Mrd DM

Bekleidung · Mineralölprodukte
Büromaschinen, EDV
Kunststoffwaren
Feinmechanik, Optik
Flugzeuge u.ä.
NE-Metalle
EBM-Waren
Textilien
Nahrungs- u. Genußmittel

5,1 · 6,3 · 6,5 · 6,8 · 7,7 · 8,1 · 9,0 · 11,0 · 13,1 · 19,5

62,6 Maschinen
62,2 Autos
52,5 Chemische Erzeugnisse
37,5 Elektrotechnik
21,0 Eisen u. Stahl

G
4254

Source: Inter Nationes

Probe-Test

A. *Translate the underlined expressions.*

1. <u>Je öfter</u> Sie Reklamen hören, <u>desto mehr</u> kaufen Sie. _____

2. Die Firmen machen Reklame, <u>um neue Käufer zu finden</u>. _____

3. Die Leute <u>leben gesünder</u>. _____

4. Das ist <u>der sicherste Weg</u> zur schlanken Linie. _____

5. <u>Keine schmeckt besser</u>. _____

6. Unsere Firmen <u>geben Millionen aus</u>. _____

B. *Complete.*

1. The comparative is formed by adding _____, and the superlative by adding

   _____.

2. A construction for the superlative often uses the word _____.

3. Adjectives in the comparative (are/are not) declined. _____

4. Adverbs in the comparative (are/are not) declined. _____

C. *Circle* True *or* False.

1. As in English, German adjectives of more than one syllable form their comparative with the equivalent of *more* (**mehr**). T   F

2. The superlative after a **der**-word is declined when it follows the noun it modifies. T   F

3. Like English, German has no irregular comparisons. T   F

4. The ending **-er** on an adjective is always a signal for the comparative. T   F

5. **so . . . wie** expresses dissimilarity. T   F

6. **je . . . je** expresses the same thing as **je . . . umso**. T   F

D. *Express in German.*

1. This car is faster. _____

2. This one is the fastest. _____

3. This one drives the fastest. _____

4. This ad is the most interesting. _____

5. But this one is still more interesting. _____

6. I like this ad best. _____

7. He has less and less time. _____

8. She dances better than you. _____

E. *Complete as suggested by the cue.*

1. (*inexpensive*) Hier ist ein _____ Auto.

2. (*cheaper*) Kaufen Sie doch ein _____ Auto!

3. (*cheapest*) Das ist unser _____ Auto.

4. (*least expensive*) Welches Auto ist _____?

5. (*less expensive*) Haben sie keine _____ Autos?

6. (*more beautiful*) Haben Sie keine _____ Wohnung?

7. (*most beautiful*) Das ist eine der _____ Wohnungen.

8. (*more beautiful*) Wir sprechen von einer _____ Wohnung.

9. (*the most beautiful*) Ihre Wohnung ist _____.

10. (*shortest*) Februar ist der _____ Monat.

11. (*shorter*) Welcher ist der _____ Monat?

12. (*shortest*) April ist nicht der _____ Monat.

13. (*shorter*) Sie meinen sicher den _____ der beiden Monate.

F. *Complete.*

1. Er trinkt Wein gern, aber Bier trinkt er _____, und Wasser trinkt er

   _____.

2. Das „Empire State Building" ist hoch, aber das „Chrysler Building" ist

   _____, und das „World Trade Center" ist

   _____.

3. Ich bin nicht so alt wie Fritz. Er ist _____, und Karl ist

   _____.

G. *Complete, using the appropriate superlative.*

1. Fritz hat viel gegessen, aber Hans _____.

2. Gerhard ist arm, aber Josef _____.

3. Ich bin gern zu Hause, aber _____ reise ich.

H. *Express in German.*

1. The ads are becoming more and more aggressive. _____

   _____

2. The less you eat, the slimmer you become. _____

   _____

3. This mistake is just as bad as this one. _____

   _____

4. This mistake is worse than this one. _____

   _____

5. I work in order to earn money. _____

   _____

6. I have nothing important to tell. _____

   _____

7. Don't let me disturb you. _____

   _____

8. Leave your car at home. _____

   _____

9. Where did you leave your car? _____

   _____

10. He had his car repaired. _____

   _____

I.   *Complete with an appropriate word from the* Lesestück.

1. Mit Perlweiß werden die _____ weißer.

2. Firmen geben Millionen aus, um neue _____ zu finden.

3. Mit einer Kanone kann man _____.

4. Gute Werbung bringt _____ Gewinne.

5. Die Werbung hilft dem Käufer besser zu _____.

6. Die Werbung _____ den Lebensstandard.

7. Der sicherste Weg zur _____ Linie ist weniger essen.

8. Mit Polaroid _____ sehen Sie besser.

9. Nasivin ist ein gutes Medikament gegen _____.

J.   *The ad writer is trying to sabotage the copy. Rewrite each sentence, replacing the inappropriate word with a better one.*

Zigaretten

1. Diese Zigarette ist im Rauch nikotinreich. _____

   _____

2. Deutschlands kürzeste Damenzigarette. _____

   _____

3. Sie ist angenehm schwer. _____

4. Keine schmeckt schlechter. _____

Getränke

5. D-Pils hat die meisten Kalorien. _____

   _____

6. Unser Kaffee ist der teuerste. _____

_____

Staubsauger

7. Unser Staubsauger hat die höchste Lautstärke. _____

_____

K. *Which words belong together? Draw lines connecting the right words.*

Staubsauger   schöner aussehen

Sonnenbrille   besser sehen

Bundeswehr   Nase

Bundesbahn   Ferien

Schnupfen   mehr als ein Job

                               Lautstärke

L. *Write an ad about your favorite or most hated product. Use comparatives and superlatives.*

_____

_____

_____

M. *An advertising executive has thought up a new gimmick to draw attention to advertising slogans. Just fill in the missing vowels and you will receive their product free.*

1. D___ f___ r g___ h___ ___ch m___ ___l___nw___ ___t.

2. P___ck d___n T___g___r ___n d___n T___nk!

3. B___ss___r s___h___n. Sch___n___r ___ ___ss___h___n.

4. T___p___sch ___m___r___k___n___sch ___m G___schm___ck.

5. W___r g___b___n ___ns m___hr M___h___!

23x Besser Schlafen!

B

Es soll Naßrasierer geben,
die noch nie einen „Gillette" verwendet haben.
Für sie wird es höchste Zeit,
jetzt „Unsere beste Rasur" kennenzulernen:
den Gillette Contour.

C

**BLEND-A-MED VERWENDER
HABEN DAS GESÜNDERE ZAHNFLEISCH**

D

Sie hat Nasivin.

Nasivin. Je früher, desto besser.
Damit Sie Ihren Schnupfen vergessen können.
Für 6–8 Stunden.

E

interRent
Deutschlands größte Autovermietung

iR

F

Immer mehr Leute haben keine Schuppen mehr.

Sind Sie auch einer der zufriedenen
Crisan-Verwender? Dann sagen Sie es
in unserer nächsten Anzeige.
Schicken Sie ein nettes Foto an
WELLA AG, Postfach 40 28,
6100 Darmstadt, Kennwort: CRISAN.

Ich habe schon
viel probiert.
Doch Crisan macht wirklich
schuppenfrei.

G

Erweitern Sie Ihren Wortschatz!

A. Englisch-Deutsch

1. toothpaste _____

2. brand (or merchandise) _____

3. railroad _____

4. trip, journey _____

5. beverage, drink _____

6. cigarette _____

7. buyer _____

8. sunglasses _____

9. sniffles, cold _____

10. television advertising _____

11. to manipulate _____

12. to bring along _____

13. to serve _____

14. to shoot _____

15. to choose _____

16. to exist _____

17. to improve _____

18. to suffice _____

19. light _____

20. stupid _____

21. healthy _____

22. full _____

23. bad, worse _____

24. the more . . . the _____

25. nothing can be changed _____

B. Deutsch-Englisch

1. die Macht _____
2. der Rauch _____
3. der Zweck _____
4. die Litfaßsäule _____
5. das Produkt _____
6. der Genuß _____
7. die Speise _____
8. die Werbung _____
9. der Tropfen _____
10. fordern _____
11. fördern _____
12. ausgeben _____
13. staubsaugen _____

14. (sich) lassen _____
15. benutzen _____
16. aussehen _____
17. vulgär _____
18. angeblich _____
19. deshalb _____
20. einzig _____
21. das stimmt nicht _____
22. solange _____
23. Na klar! _____
24. je früher, desto . . . _____
25. sein Bestes geben _____

Hör zu . . .und antworte!   Antwortbogen

Übung **A**.   *Circle A, B, or C. Sometimes more than one answer is correct.*

1. A   B   C   2. A   B   C   3. A   B   C   4. A   B   C

5. A   B   C   6. A   B   C

Übung **B**.   *Circle A, B, or C.*

1. A   B   C   2. A   B   C   3. A   B   C   4. A   B   C

5. A   B   C   6. A   B   C   7. A   B   C   8. A   B   C

9. A   B   C   10. A   B   C

See Übung C, page 190,
Owen Franken/Stock, Boston

Kapitel 12   **189**

Übung **C.** *Circle* **Richtig** *or* **Falsch**.

1. R   F   2. R   F   3. R   F   4. R   F   5. R   F   6. R   F

7. R   F   8. R   F   9. R   F   10. R   F   11. R   F   12. R   F

13. R   F   14. R   F   15. R   F   16. R   F   17. R   F   18. R   F

19. R   F   20. R   F   21. R   F   22. R   F   23. R   F   24. R   F

25. R   F

Übung **D.** *Circle A or B, or both.*

1. A   B   2. A   B   3. A   B   4. A   B   5. A   B   6. A   B

7. A   B   8. A   B   9. A   B   10. A   B

Übung **E.** **Diktat**

1. _____

2. _____

3. _____

Kapitel 13

Selbst-Test

DIALOG

Translate the underlined expressions.

1. Sind Sie der junge Mann, <u>der sich</u> um die Stelle <u>bewirbt</u>?   — who is applying
2. Ich möchte Kontakt mit Menschen. <u>Den wünsch' ich mir</u>.   — I wish for that.
3. Ich will keinen Job, <u>bei dem man nur sitzt</u>.   — where one only sits
4. In der Schule, <u>die ich besuchte</u>, gab es das nicht.   — which I attended
5. <u>Das macht nichts</u>.   — It does not matter.

1. Relative pronouns

6. Relative pronouns are similar to the (definite/indefinite) articles.   — definite
7. They have the same gender and _____ as the _____ to which they refer.   — number, noun
8. They always cause (V-S/V-L) word order.   — V-L
9. Their _____ depends on their function in the dependent clause.   — case
10. Relative clauses are always set off by _____.   — commas
11. Relative pronouns (can/cannot) be omitted in German.   — cannot
12. The relative pronouns are declined like the definite article, except for (four/five) "long" forms.   — five
13. These forms occur in all forms of the (dative/genitive), and in the _____ _____.   — genitive, dative plural
14. The "long" forms add _____ to the definite article.   — **en** (or **-sen**)

Complete with the appropriate relative pronoun.

15. Ich kenne ein Kaufhaus, _____ billig ist.   — das
16. Ich habe eine Versicherung, _____ sehr gut ist.   — die
17. Ich kenne einen Kunden, _____ es kaufen wird.   — der

18. Ich kenne viele Kunden, _____ sich dafür interessieren. — die
19. Die Frau, _____ Sie dort sehen, ist die Leiterin. — die
20. Der Abiturient, _____ Sie interviewen wollen, ist hier. — den
21. Das Büro, _____ Sie suchen, ist dort. — das
22. Die Leute, _____ Sie interviewen möchten, sind hier. — die
23. Der junge Mann, _____ Sie geholfen haben, ist am Telefon. — dem
24. Die Leiterin, _____ Sie geschrieben haben, ist auf Urlaub. — der
25. Das Fräulein, _____ der Regenschirm gehört, hat angerufen. — dem
26. Die zwei Abiturienten, _____ Sie geschrieben haben, kommen
    heute um 9 Uhr. — denen
27. Wie heißt der Abiturient, _____ Adresse wir nicht haben? — dessen
28. Wie heißt die Abiturientin, _____ Empfehlungsschreiben so
    gut war? — deren
29. Das Kaufhaus, _____ Reklamen so gut sind, ist jetzt
    bankrott. — dessen
30. Die Kunden, _____ Rechnungen nicht bezahlt sind, dürfen
    nichts mehr kaufen. — deren

31. In German, when a preposition is used with a relative
    pronoun, the preposition may (sometimes/never) come at
    the end of the clause. — never

Insert the prepositions for *and* **für** *in the correct place to complete
the sentences.*

32. Die Firma, die er arbeitet, verkauft Jeans. — ... Firma, für
    die ....

33. *The company he works sells jeans.* — ... *works for
    sells ....*

Complete, arranging the cue words in the proper order.

34. (warte/auf/den/ich) Der Brief, _____ _____ _____
    _____, ist noch nicht angekommen. — auf den ich warte
35. (der/ich/wohne/bei) Die Familie, _____ _____ _____
    _____, ist sehr nett. — bei der ich wohne
36. (dem/ich/das Auto/habe/gekauft/von) Der Amerikaner,

    _____ _____ _____ _____ _____ _____ _____,

    heißt Joe Blow. — von dem ich das
    Auto gekauft habe

2. The indefinite relative pronouns **wer** and **was**

37. **Wer** as a relative pronoun may mean *who,* _____, or
    _____ _____.

    — *whoever, he who*

38. **Was** as a relative pronoun may mean *what,* _____, or
    _____ _____.

    — *whatever, that which*

39. Both are used as relative pronouns when there is no
    (antecedent person or thing/antecedent person/ antecedent
    thing).

    — antecedent person or
    thing

40. They are also used when the antecedent is _____ or is
    a whole clause.

    — nonspecific

Complete with **wer** *or* **was,** *and give its English equivalent.*

41. _____ Geld hat, hat Glück.
42. Sie können machen, _____ Sie wollen.
43. _____ Sie sagen, ist richtig.
44. _____ das sagt, ist ein Dummkopf.

— Wer (*Whoever*)
— was (*whatever*)
— Was (*Whatever*)
— Wer (*Whoever*)

3. **wo** as a relative pronoun

45. **Wo** is often used to replace a preposition + relative
    pronoun when referring to a _____.

    — place

Restate, replacing **wo** *with a preposition + personal pronoun, or
vice versa, when appropriate.*

46. Die Konditorei, wo wir uns treffen, ist sehr gemütlich. Die
    Konditorei, _____ wir uns treffen, ist sehr gemütlich.

    — in der

47. Hier ist das Geschäft, in dem ich arbeite. Hier ist das
    Geschäft, _____ ich arbeite.

    — wo

48. Wien ist die Stadt, in der ich am liebsten lebe. Wien ist die
    Stadt, _____ ich am liebsten lebe.

    — wo

49. A preposition + the indefinite pronoun **was** may be re-
    placed by a _____-compound.

    — **wo**

Replace the preposition and indefinite pronoun with a **wo**-
compound.

50. Ist das das Auto, für das du dich interessierst? Ist das das
    Auto, _____ du dich interessierst?

    — wofür

51. Das ist das Telegramm, auf das sie solange wartete. Das ist
    das Telegramm, _____ sie so lange wartete.

    — worauf

52. Das Problem, über das wir sprachen, ist ernst. Das Problem,
    _____ wir sprachen, ist ernst.

    — worüber

4. Demonstrative pronouns

53. Demonstrative pronouns are the definite articles and _____ in all its forms.

— **dieser**

54. A demonstrative pronoun (describes/points out) an item that is part of a larger collection.

— points out

55. The declension of demonstrative pronouns is the same as that of the (definite article/relative pronoun).

— relative pronoun

56. In speaking, the demonstrative pronouns are always _____.

— stressed

Complete with the appropriate form of the demonstrative pronoun derived from **der, die, das.**

57. Dieser Platz ist besser als _____ da.

— der

58. In dem Campingplatz hier sind weniger Leute als in _____ dort.

— dem

59. Ich möchte dieses Zelt dort, nicht _____ da.

— das

60. Wir sprechen nicht von diesen Touristen hier, sondern von _____ dort.

— denen

Complete with the appropriate form of **dies-** *used as a demonstrative pronoun.*

61. Haben Sie solche Postkarten? —Ja, _____ haben wir.

— diese

62. Ich möchte eine mit einem Foto, aber nicht mit _____ hier.

— diesem

63. Ja, das Foto gefällt mir besser als _____ da.

— dieses (*or* dies)

64. The short form **dies** may be used in the _____ case for all genders, singular and plural.

— nominative

65. The neuter pronoun **das** may be used for all _____ in the singular and plural.

— nouns

66. It may also be used for a whole _____.

— clause

Complete with **dies** *or* **das**, *and give its English equivalent.*

67. _____ ist mein Koffer.

— Dies *or* Das (*This*)

68. Das ist meine Schwester, und _____ hier sind meine Eltern.

— dies (*these*)

69. Der Amerikaner dort? _____ ist mein neuer Freund.

— Das (*That*)

70. Ja, _____ waren Zeiten!

— das (*these*)

71. Wer ist die Dame dort? _____ ist die neue Chefin.

— Das (*That*)

72. The difference between a relative pronoun and a demonstrative pronoun can be determined from (its declension/word order).

— word order

Supply a relative or demonstrative pronoun, and give its English equivalent.

    73. Du, das Moped, _____ mir gefällt, ist schon verkauft.   — das (*which*)

    74. Du, dein Moped, _____ gefällt mir!   — das (*that one*)

5. The prefixes **un-** and **ur-** and the suffixes **-bar** and **-los**

Translate the underlined words.

    75. Ja, das war <u>eine ungemütliche Situation</u>.   — *an unpleasant situation*

    76. In dieser stillen Laube <u>sind wir ungestört</u>.   — *we are not disturbed*

    77. Das ist ein großes <u>Unglück</u>.   — *misfortune*

    78. Wo gibt es noch heute einen <u>Urwald</u>?   — *primeval forest*

    79. Das ist ein <u>uraltes</u> Problem.   — *very old, ancient*

    80. Er ist <u>leblos</u>.   — *lifeless*

    81. Das ist <u>undenkbar</u>!   — *unthinkable*

Complete on the basis of the Lesestück.

    82. Fast jeder, der eine Stelle sucht, muß einen _____ schreiben.   — Lebenslauf

    83. Man geht zuerst auf die _____ und dann auf das Gymnasium.   — Volksschule

    84. Auf einer Universität studiert man ein _____.   — Hauptfach

    85. Mit einem Stipendium bekommt man _____.   — Geld

    86. Man kann sich nur an einer Universität _____, wenn man das Abitur hat.   — immatrikulieren

    87. Ein Grundstückmakler (oder eine Maklerin) verkauft _____.   — Häuser

    88. In Deutschland geht man zuerst auf die _____ und dann auf die _____ und dann auf die Hochschule.   — Volksschule, Oberschule

    89. Ein Sport, den man besonders liebt, ist ein _____.   — Lieblingssport

    90. Das Essen, das man am liebsten hat, ist das _____.   — Lieblingsessen

    91. Mein deutsches Lieblingsessen ist _____.   — ?

Probe-Test

A. *Translate the underlined expressions.*

1. Ich studiere in Graz, <u>wo ich ein Stipendium bekommen habe</u>. _____

   _____

2. <u>Neben meinem Studium</u> spiele ich Klarinette in einem Nachtklub. _____

   _____

3. Im Sommer 1983 <u>arbeitete ich als Dolmetscherin</u>. _____

   _____

4. In den Ferien, <u>die ich am liebsten in den Bergen verbringe</u>, wandere ich gern. _____

   _____

5. Der Alpenverein, <u>dessen Mitglied ich bin</u>, ist wie der amerikanische Sierra Club. _____

   _____

B. 1. Relative pronouns have the same gender and number as _____

   _____.

2. Their case is determined by _____

   _____.

C. Complete with the correct form of the relative pronoun.

1. Mein Vater, _____ seit 20 Jahren für die Post arbeitet, ist in Mansfield geboren.

2. Meine Mutter, _____ Familie aus dem Süden stammt, ist Lehrerin.

3. Meine jüngere Schwester, _____ in die Oberschule geht, wohnt noch zu Hause.

4. Biologie ist ein Fach, für _____ ich mich sehr interessiere.

5. Letzten Sommer, _____ ich zu Hause verbrachte, arbeitete ich bei einer Baufirma.

6. Skateboardfahren, mit _____ ich erst im College begonnen habe, ist mein Hobby.

7. Mein Biologielehrer, _____ Unterricht ich besonders gut fand, hat mich beeinflußt.

8. Meine Deutschlehrerin, mit _____ ich eine Deutschlandreise gemacht habe, lehrt auch Geschichte an unserer Schule.

D. Complete, putting the cue words into the proper word order.

1. (verbringe/am liebsten/in den Bergen/die/ich)

   In den Ferien, _____

   _____, wandere ich gern.

2. (an einem College/der/studiert)

   Das ist der Lebenslauf eines jungen Amerikaners, _____

   _____

3. (beim genauen Lesen/erkennen/die/kann/man)

   Es gibt Unterschiede, _____

   _____

E. Combine the two sentences with the help of a relative pronoun.

1. Das ist die Heiratsannonce. Ich habe auf die Heiratsannonce geantwortet.

   _____

2. Wie heißt der Mann? Du hast sein Foto bekommen.

_____

3. Das ist ein Typ. Ich möchte ihn nicht heiraten.

_____

4. Hier ist ein Brief von einem Mädchen. Es ist mir sehr sympathisch.

_____

5. Was schreibt der Junge? Er ist dir unsympathisch.

_____

F. 1. The indefinite relative pronouns are _____ and _____.

2. Wo can also function as a relative pronoun instead of _____

_____.

3. Wo must be used when referring to _____.

4. Wo-compounds are used to replace a preposition + _____

_____.

G. *Translate.*

1. Wer an einer Hochschule studieren will, muß das Abitur haben.

_____

2. Was nicht richtig ist, ist falsch.

_____

H. *Complete with* wo, was, *or* wer.

1. Das, _____ ich gelernt habe, ist interessant.

2. Klagenfurt ist die Stadt, _____ ich mein Arbitur gemacht habe.

3. _____ nicht für diese Politik ist, ist dagegen.

I. *Replace the preposition and relative pronoun with a **wo**-compound.*

   1. Skateboardfahren, mit dem ich erst jetzt begonnen habe, gefällt mir gut.

   _____

   _____

   2. Das Fußballspiel, auf das ich mich freue, ist nächste Woche.

   _____

J. *Express in German.*

   1. This is my car. _____

   2. This nightclub is more expensive than that one there. _____

   _____

K. *Complete, using a relative clause with or without a preposition.*

   1. Das ist ein Film, _____

   2. Die Musik, _____, gefällt mir

   am besten.

   3. Das Buch, _____, war nicht

   interessant.

   4. Mein Hauptfach, _____

L. *Draw lines connecting the clauses to create a statement that makes sense.*

Es war meine Entscheidung,   verbringe ich meine Ferien in den Bergen.

In meiner Freizeit   Wissenschaftler

Da ich mich um eine Stelle bewerbe,   höre ich gern Musik.

Vielleicht werde ich   spiele ich mit meinem Schäferhund.

Als Mitglied des Alpenvereins,   Biologie zu studieren.

                                               schreibe ich meinen Lebenslauf.

M. *Select the correct antonym from the list below.*

ausgeben   verbringen   aufhören   lernen   nie

1. oft _____

2. verdienen _____

3. beginnen _____

4. lehren _____

N. *Write your own short curriculum vitae. Include in it information about the following items.*

a) your family   c) leisure-time activities and hobbies
b) schooling (past and present)   d) plans for the future

_____

_____

_____

_____

_____

O. *Complete with statements that apply to your own experience.*

1. Ein Job-Interview macht mir immer Angst, weil _____

   _____

   _____

   _____

   ich sehr nervös bin.
   ich nicht weiß, was ich sagen soll.
   ich wirklich nicht für diesen Job qualifiziert bin.
   ich kein Deutsch kann.
   die Fragen mir auf die Nerven gehen.
   ich die Nase voll habe.

2. Ein Job-Interview macht mir keine Angst, weil _____

   _____

   _____

   _____

   ich weiß, was ich will.
   ich es auf die leichte Schulter nehme.
   ich für den Job qualifiziert bin.
   ich lebe, um zu arbeiten und nicht arbeite, um zu leben.
   ich einen B.A. habe.
   der Cousin meiner geschiedenen Mutter (meines geschiedenen Vaters) der Onkel des Direktors dieser
       multinationalen Firma ist.

Erweitern Sie Ihren Wortschatz!

A. Englisch-Deutsch

1. department store _____

2. secretary _____

3. curriculum vitae _____

4. course, class _____

5. member _____

6. summer _____

7. letter of recommendation _____

_____

8. working hours _____

9. scholarship _____

10. elementary school _____

11. instruction, teaching _____

_____

12. desk _____

13. skier *f* _____

14. to type _____

15. to influence _____

16. to suggest _____

17. to sing _____

18. to apply _____

19. to register (at university) _____

20. born _____

21. classical _____

22. behind _____

23. several _____

24. to attend school _____

25. Congratulations! _____

B. Deutsch-Englisch

1. das Hauptfach _____

2. die Bewerbung _____

3. das Gehalt _____

4. die Geschwister _____

5. die Note _____

6. die Versicherung _____

7. der Schäferhund _____

8. die Verbesserung _____

   _____

9. der Unterschied _____

10. das Gymnasium _____

11. der Kundendienst _____

12. der Schutz _____

13. die Hochschule _____

14. die Schwester _____

15. stammen (aus) _____

16. verbringen _____

17. kämpfen _____

18. sammeln _____

19. gratulieren _____

20. ähnlich _____

21. jedenfalls _____

22. geradeaus _____

23. Nehmen Sie Platz! _____

24. auf Wunsch _____

25. neben dem Studium _____

Hör zu...und antworte!   Antwortbogen

Übung **A**.   *Circle A, B, or C.*

1. A B C   2. A B C   3. A B C   4. A B C

5. A B C   6. A B C   7. A B C   8. A B C

Übung **B**.   *Circle* **Richtig** *or* **Falsch.**

1. R F   2. R F   3. R F   4. R F   5. R F   6. R F

7. R F   8. R F   9. R F

Übung **C**.   *Circle* **Richtig** *or* **Falsch.**

1. R F   2. R F   3. R F   4. R F   5. R F   6. R F

7. R F   8. R F   9. R F   10. R F   11. R F   12. R F

13. R F   14. R F   15. R F   16. R F

Übung **D**.   *Write down another word belonging to the same category.*

1. _____   2. _____   3. _____   4. _____

5. _____   6. _____

Übung **E.** *Circle A or B.*

1. A   B   2. A   B   3. A   B   4. A   B   5. A   B   6. A   B

7. A   B   8. A   B

Kapitel 14

Selbst-Test

DIALOG

Translate the underlined expressions.

1. Die Astronauten <u>waren gelandet</u>.
2. Erinnern Sie sich noch, was Armstrong <u>gesagt hatte</u>?
3. Die Satelliten, <u>die man entwickelt hatte</u>, helfen bei der Wettervorhersage.

4. <u>Muß immer alles „entweder—oder" sein?</u>

— had landed
— had said

— which had been developed
— Must everything always be "either—or"?

1. The past perfect tense

5. The past perfect tense is formed in the same way as the present perfect tense, except that it uses the _____ tense of **haben** or **sein**.
6. The past tense of **haben** is **Ich** _____.
7. The past tense of **sein** is **Ich** _____.
8. The past perfect is formed with the past tense of **haben** or **sein** + the _____ _____.
9. The past perfect in German is used (very often/not very often).
10. It must be used when describing an event that took place before another _____ event.

— past
— **hatte**
— **war**

— past participle

— not very often

— past

Supply the past tense of the auxiliary to complete the past perfect statement.

11. Schliemann _____ schon Russisch gelernt, als er nach St. Petersburg fuhr.

— hatte

12. Bald nachdem Schliemann nach Rußland gefahren _____, wurde er sehr erfolgreich.

— war

Supply the past participle of the cue verb.

13. (erfinden) Sobald die DDR den „Staatsamateur" _____ hatte, ist sie zur Großmacht im Sport geworden.

— erfunden

14. (werden) Aus dem geplanten Programm war Wirklichkeit _____.

— geworden

15. (sehen) Die DDR hatte Erfolge, wie sie die Welt noch nie _____ hatte.

— gesehen

In the following sentences, the conjugated verb is in the present perfect. What would the verb be in the past perfect?

16. Ich habe die Geschichte von Troja schon oft gehört.

— hatte . . . gehört

17. Ich habe sie als Kind gelesen.

— hatte . . . gelesen

18. Und dann habe ich gelernt, daß Schliemann nach Griechenland gefahren ist.

— hatte . . . gelernt, gefahren war

19. Dort hat er Troja entdeckt.

— hatte . . . entdeckt

20. In the past perfect tense the separable prefix of a verb (is/ is not) joined with the stem verb in the past participle.

— is

Restate, transforming the verb into the past perfect.

21. Ich stand gestern um acht Uhr auf. Ich _____.

— war gestern um acht Uhr aufgestanden

22. Er sagt, daß er gestern um acht Uhr anrief. Er sagt, daß _____.

— er gestern um acht Uhr angerufen hatte

23. Ich wußte nicht, daß du schon gestern angekommen bist. Ich wußte nicht, daß du _____.

— schon gestern angekommen warst

24. Er fuhr schon vor einer Woche nach Dänemark ab. Er _____.

— war schon vor einer Woche nach Dänemark abgefahren

2. More on compound nouns

25. German compound nouns take their gender from the (initial/final) component.

— final

26. Sometimes a linking _____, _____, or _____ is inserted between the components.

— -s-, -es-, -n-

Combine the two words to form a compound noun. Then give its English equivalent.

27. der Raum *space*   die Fahrt *travel* _____   — die Raumfahrt
                                                             (*space travel*)

28. die Rakete *rocket*   die Forschung *research* _____   — die Raketenforschung
                                                             (*rocket research*)

29. der Mond *moon*   die Landung *landing* _____   — die Mondlandung
                                                             (*moon landing*)

30. das Land *land*   die Wirtschaft *economy* _____   — die Landwirtschaft
                                                             (*agriculture*)

31. die Kindheit *childhood*   der Traum *dream* _____   — der Kindheitstraum
                                                             (*childhood dream*)

32. der Riese *giant*   der Sprung *leap* _____   — der Riesensprung
                                                             (*giant leap*)

3. Noun suffixes

33. Nouns formed with the suffixes **-ung, -heit, -keit, -schaft**
    are always _____ in gender.   — feminine

34. They often correspond to the English suffixes _____, _____,
    _____, _____, _____, _____, and _____.   — -tion, -ity, -ness,
                                                              -hood, -ing, -dom,
                                                              -ship

Give the German equivalent and the definite article.

35. *freedom*   _____   — die Freiheit

36. *invention*   _____   — die Erfindung

37. *possibility* _____   — die Möglichkeit

38. *childhood*   _____   — die Kindheit

39. *friendship* _____   — die Freundschaft

40. *sickness*   _____   — die Krankheit

41. Most nouns ending in **-tum** are _____ in gender.   — neuter
42. Two exceptions are _____ in gender.   — masculine

Give the German equivalent and the definite article.

43. *property* _____   — das Eigentum
44. *error*   _____   — der Irrtum
45. *wealth*   _____   — der Reichtum
46. *growth*   _____   — das Wachstum

4. Inseparable prefixes

47. The seven most common inseparable prefixes are: _____,
    _____, _____, _____, _____, _____, and _____.   — be-, emp-, ent-, er,
                                                              ge-, ver-, zer-

48. (No/Some) inseparable prefixes have an independent
    meaning.   — Some

49. The prefix **be-** turns (a transitive/an intransitive) verb
    into (a transitive/an intransitive) verb.   — an intransitive,
                                                              a transitive

50. **ent-** usually suggests (separation/combination).   — separation
51. **er-** usually denotes (beginning/completion) of an action. — completion
52. **ver-** may suggest something (well done/gone wrong).   — gone wrong
53. **zer-** (always/sometimes) denotes disintegration.   — always
54. Only three verbs use the inseparable prefix **emp-** They are:
    to receive _____, **empfehlen** *to* _____, and *to feel* _____.   — **empfangen**,
                                                              recommend,
                                                              empfinden

55. **laufen** means *to run*, **entlaufen** means *to* _____. — *run away*
56. **trinken** means *to drink*, **ertrinken** means *to* _____. — *drown*
57. **brechen** means *to break*, **zerbrechen** means *to* _____. — *break to pieces*

*Complete with the appropriate inseparable prefix verb suggested by
the content. Then give its English equivalent.*

58. Hitler war „Der Führer", aber er hat das deutsche Volk
    _____.   — *verführt (misled)*

59. Bei Null Grad kann man frieren, aber bei Minus 40 Grad
    kann man _____.   — *erfrieren (freeze to
                                                              death)*

60. Es ist leicht, etwas zu kaufen, aber es ist nicht so leicht,
    etwas zu _____.   — *verkaufen (sell)*
61. Schlafen ist schön, aber _____ kann den Job kosten.   — *verschlafen (over-
                                                              sleeping)*

62. Revolver können schießen, aber nur Menschen können
    andere Menschen _____.   — *erschießen (kill by
                                                              shooting)*

63. Raten macht Spaß, aber _____ macht noch mehr Spaß!   — *erraten (to guess
                                                              correctly)*

5. Cognates

64. Cognates are words in related languages that have the same
    (origin/meaning).   — origin
65. There are (seven/nine) consonant "sound shifts."   — seven

66. The English consonants that are related to German
    consonants are: _____, _____, _____, _____, _____,
    _____, and _____.   — p, t, k, d, th, v (f), y

Give the corresponding cognate consonants in English.

67. German **f, ff, pf**   English _____   — p
68. German **z, ß**   English _____   — t
69. German **ch**   English _____   — k
70. German **t**   English _____   — d
71. German **d**   English _____   — th
72. German **b**   English _____ or _____   — v, f
73. German **g**   English _____   — y

*Can you guess the English meaning of the following German
cognates?*

74. Pfennig _____, Zeit _____, backen _____   — penny, tide, to bake
75. das Ding _____, der Hund _____, die Stube _____   — thing, hound, stove
76. die Distel _____, der Apfel _____, der Tropfen _____ — thistle, apple, drop
77. der Witz _____, hoffen _____, das Salz _____   — wit, to hope, salt
78. kochen _____, die Leber _____, streben _____   — to cook, liver, to
                                                            strive
79. das Kalb _____, das Leder _____, das Blatt _____ — calf, leather, blade
80. das Schwert _____, die Saat _____, der Fuß _____ — sword, seed, foot

Complete on the basis of the Lesestück. *More than one choice may
be correct.*

81. Seine Mutter (schenkte/gab) ihm ein Teleskop.   — both are possible
82. Er wurde Mitglied einer (Rakete/Gesellschaft).   — Gesellschaft
83. Er (verbrachte/landete) viel Zeit auf dem Feld.   — verbrachte
84. Schwere Waffen durfte man nicht (bauen/entwickeln). — both are possible
85. Raketen waren (erlaubt/verboten).   — verboten
86. Die Mondlandung _____ viel Geld.   — kostete
87. Ich weiß, daß Sie es nicht _____.   — können
88. Gebt uns die _____!   — Mittel
89. Die Armee wollte eine neue Waffe _____.   — entwickeln
90. Die wertvollen Fische gingen gern in _____.   — das Netz

Probe-Test

A. *Translate the underlined expressions.*

1. <u>Als er später Physik studierte,</u> wurde er Mitglied. _____

   _____

2. <u>Er verbrachte jede freie Minute</u> auf dem Feld, wo man mit Raketen experimentierte.

   _____

3. <u>Obwohl er</u> für die Armee <u>arbeitete, hatte er</u> sein Lieblingsprojekt <u>nie vergessen.</u>

   _____

4. Vielleicht <u>hatte schon</u> damals sein Dilemma <u>begonnen.</u> _____

B. *Restate, putting the verb into the past perfect.*

1. Er denkt immer nur an Geld.

   _____

2. Während unserer Ferien ist das Wetter immer schlecht.

   _____

3. Sie hat sich für Politik interessiert.

   _____

4. Er sagte, daß die Züge immer pünktlich ankommen.

_____

5. Wann warst du in Österreich?

_____

6. Warum arbeitest du Tag und Nacht?

_____

7. Der Traum wird Wirklichkeit.

_____

C. _Combine the two sentences, putting the verb in the first into the past, and the verb in the second into the past perfect._

Use **denn** _as the conjunction._

1. Röntgen ist glücklich. Er hat den Nobelpreis erhalten.

Röntgen _____

_____

2. Er verdient ihn. Er hat sein ganzes Leben dafür gearbeitet.

Er _____

_____

3. Er freut sich. Viele Studenten sind zu ihm gekommen.

Er _____

_____

Now use **weil** *as the conjunction.*

4. Professor Pierre Curie bekommt den Nobelpreis. Seine Frau Marie Curie hat ihm geholfen.

   Professor Pierre Curie _____

   _____

5. Beide erhalten den Nobelpreis. Beide hatten die Entdeckung zusammen gemacht.

   Beide _____

   _____

D. *Express in German.*

1. I had not known it. _____

2. I have known it. _____

3. I was there. _____

4. I had been there. _____

E. *Form compound nouns and give their English equivalent.*

	COMPOUND NOUN	ENGLISH EQUIVALENT
1. der Urlaub, die Reise	_____	_____
2. schreiben, die Maschine	_____	_____
3. der Tag, die Temperatur	_____	_____
4. fort, der Schritt	_____	_____
5. der Hunger, die Not	_____	_____

F. *Antworten Sie auf deutsch!*

1. Was haben die Brüder Grimm gesammelt?

   _____

2. Welche Sprachen haben sie verglichen?

_____

3. Was haben sie durch ihre Forschung erkannt?

_____

4. Was kann man im „Deutschen Wörterbuch" von den Brüdern Grimm finden?

_____

5. Was müssen alle Kandidaten für den PhD in Englisch lernen?

_____

G. *Complete with the correct word from the list below.*

Küche	Arm	während	ißt
Haus	Hund	weil	frißt
Fuß	Wolf	küßt	Schloß

1. Rotkäppchen hat keine Angst vor dem großen bösen _____.

2. Der Prinz findet Aschenputtel, weil sie den kleinsten _____ hat.

3. Schneewittchen schläft, bis der Prinz sie wieder wach _____.

4. Die sieben Zwerge helfen Schneewittchen, _____ sie schläft.

5. Der böse Wolf _____ die Großmutter auf.

6. Aschenputtel muß in der _____ arbeiten.

H. *Read and answer the questions below in German.*

Nach dem zweiten Weltkrieg wollten die Vereinigten Staaten den Menschen in West-
deutschland helfen. Ostdeutschland, die heutige DDR, war natürlich gegen diese
Hilfe aus dem kapitalistischen Amerika. Die amerikanische Regierung aber wollte den
Deutschen zeigen, wie großzügig° die Amerikaner sind. Und wie zeigte man das? — generous
Viele große Kisten° mit Maschinen und anderen Materialien aus Amerika kamen in — crates
Bremerhaven an. In den Zeitungen Westdeutschlands sah man viele Fotos davon.
Auch in den ostdeutschen Zeitungen gab es Fotos von den Kisten. Aber unter den

Fotos stand: „Kommentar überflüssig°". Für eine antikapitalistische Propaganda brauchte man keinen Kommentar: Auf jeder Kiste stand in großen schwarzen Buchstaben°:

not necessary, superfluous

black letters

1. Was wollten die Vereinigten Staaten nach dem Krieg tun? _____

_____

2. Was kam in Bremerhaven an? _____

_____

3. Was sah man in vielen Zeitungen Westdeutschlands? _____

_____

4. Warum war ein Kommentar in den Zeitungen der DDR „überflüssig"? _____

_____

I. **Worüber man in Deutschland lacht**

Two astronauts, a Russian and an American, meet in outer space. As they pass each other, one says: „Fritz, was machst du denn hier oben?" The other replies: „Na, Karl, dasselbe wie du damals in Peenemünde!"

Answer the questions in German.

1. Worin liegt der Witz? Der Witz, liegt darin, daß _____

_____

2. Warum freuen sich die Deutschen über diesen Witz? Sie freuen sich weil, _____

_____

Worüber lacht man . . .

1
in Deutschland
Courtesy Elefantenpress-Karicartoon '81, Berlin

MUSIC

2 in Österreich
Courtesy *Wiener Kurier.*

Wetter-, Nachrichten- oder Sportbulletin?

3 in der Schweiz
Courtesy ''Weltwoche,'' Zurich.

1. Die erste Karikatur zeigt _____

_____

_____

2. Die zweite zeigt _____

_____

3. Die dritte zeigt _____

_____

_____

Erweitern Sie Ihren Wortschatz!

A. Englisch-Deutsch

1. call (*telephone*) _____

2. moon _____

3. science _____

4. politics, policy _____

5. outer space _____

6. task _____

7. bicycle _____

8. song _____

9. troops _____

10. climate _____

11. technician, engineer _____

12. space travel _____

13. courage _____

14. God _____

15. army _____

16. to be worth _____

17. to explain _____

18. to give (*a present*) _____

19. to catch _____

20. to plan _____

21. to experiment _____

22. great, terrific _____

23. just great! _____

24. to come to power _____

25. it did not take long _____

_____

B. Deutsch-Englisch

1. der Sprecher _____

2. die Luftverschmutzung _____

3. die Milliarde _____

4. der Hörer _____

5. der Riesensprung _____

6. der Frieden _____

7. die Gesellschaft _____

8. der Konstrukteur _____

9. die Leistung _____

10. das Wetten _____

11. die Forschung _____

12. die Vorwahl _____

13. die Rakete _____

14. das Netz _____

15. verbieten _____

16. bewundern _____

17. entwickeln _____

18. lösen _____

19. dauern _____

20. vorwärts _____

21. geheim _____

22. seit langem _____

23. nachdem _____

24. recht geben _____

25. entweder . . . oder _____

_____

NAME _____ KURS _____ DATUM _____

Hör zu . . .und antworte!   Antwortbogen

Übung **A**. *Circle* **Logisch** *or* **Unsinn**.

1. L   U   2. L   U   3. L   U   4. L   U   5. L   U   6. L   U

Übung **B**. *Write down the word that does not fit.*

1. _____   2. _____   3. _____   4. _____

5. _____   6. _____

Übung **C**. *Circle A, B, or C.*

1. A   B   C   2. A   B   C   3. A   B   C   4. A   B   C

5. A   B   C   6. A   B   C   7. A   B   C   8. A   B   C

9. A   B   C   10. A   B   C   11. A   B   C   12. A   B   C

Übung **D**. *Circle A or B.*

1. A   B   2. A   B   3. A   B   4. A   B   5. A   B   6. A   B

Übung **E.** *Circle* **Ja** *or* **Nein.**

1. Ja   Nein   2. Ja   Nein   3. Ja   Nein   4. Ja   Nein   5. Ja   Nein

6. Ja   Nein   7. Ja   Nein   8. Ja   Nein

Kapitel 15

Selbst-Test

DIALOG

Translate the underlined expressions.

1. Wenn ich nur schon größer wäre!
— If only I were already bigger!

2. Wenn ich nur mehr Geld hätte!
— If only I had more money!

3. Wenn sie/er mich nur lieben würde!
— If only she/he loved me!

4. Ich wünschte, es gäbe keine Inflation.
— I wish there were

5. Hätte ich nur mehr Zeit!
— If I had

6. Wären wir doch schon pensioniert!
— If only we were

1. The general subjunctive

7. The indicative mood describes _____.
— reality

8. The subjunctive mood often communicates _____.
— unreality

9. The "unreality" communicated by the subjunctive may be wishes, _____, _____, and _____.
— suppositions, conjectures, conditions contrary to fact

10. The subjunctive has (two/six) time frames.
— two

11. One time frame functions for the present or the _____, the other for the _____.
— future, past

12. The English subjunctive form that corresponds to *I know* is *I* _____; for *I will* it is *I* _____; for *I can* it is *I* _____.
— *knew, would, could*

13. The general subjunctive of weak verbs in the present/future time frame uses the same forms as those of the indicative _____ tense.
— past

14. The general subjunctive of a weak verb can therefore only be distinguished from the past indicative by the (ending/context).

— context

Complete the English equivalent.

15. Wenn ich Geld hätte, kaufte ich mir ein Auto. *If I _____ money, I _____ myself a car.*

— *had, would buy*

16. Vor der Inflation kaufte ich mir alle zwei Jahre ein neues Auto. *Before the inflation, I _____ a new car every two years.*

— *bought (myself)*

17. Letztes Jahr rauchtest du viel mehr. *Last year you _____ much more.*

— *smoked*

18. Ich dachte, du rauchtest jetzt nicht mehr. *I _____ you no longer _____.*

— *thought, smoked*

19. The general subjunctive of mixed and strong verbs, as well as of weak verbs, is derived from the (present/past) tense.

— past

20. The personal endings for the general subjunctive of weak, mixed, and strong verbs are (different from/the same as) those of the past tense.

— the same as

21. In the general subjunctive, the two differences between weak verbs on the one hand, and mixed or strong verbs on the other, are: Strong and mixed verbs have no dental suffix _____ between the stem and the personal ending.

— -t-

22. Strong and mixed verbs _____ the stem vowel when it is **a, o,** or **u.**

— umlaut

23. The personal endings of both the indicative past tense and the general subjunctive are: _____, _____, _____, _____, _____, _____.

— -e, -est, -e, -en, -et, -en

24. The **-e-** is often omitted in the _____-form and the _____-form.

— du, ihr

Supply the missing forms.

	INFINITIVE	PAST TENSE	GENERAL SUBJUNCTIVE	
25.	haben	ich _____	ich _____	— hatte, hätte
26.	sein	er _____	er _____	— war, wäre
27.	machen	du _____	du _____	— machtest, machtest
28.	sprechen	wir _____	wir _____	— sprachen, sprächen
29.	können	sie (*they*) _____	sie _____	— konnten, könnten
30.	gehen	ihr _____	ihr _____	— ginget, ginget

Complete with the appropriate general subjunctive form of the cue infinitive.

31. (spielen) Wenn er doch nur besser _____!   — spielte
32. (sein) _____ du nur immer so pünktlich wie heute!   — Wärest
33. (vergessen) Wenn ich nur nicht immer die Antwort _____!   — vergäße
34. (denken) Wenn Karl nur nicht so schlecht von mir _____!   — dächte
35. (haben) Wenn wir doch nur schönes Wetter _____!   — hätten
36. (bekommen) Wenn ihr nur nicht so viele
    Hausaufgaben _____!   — bekämet

2. würde + infinitive as a substitute for the subjunctive

37. The verb from which **würde** is derived is _____.   — **werden**
38. Any form of **würde** always corresponds to English _____.   — *would*
39. There is a growing tendency in German to use **würde** plus
    the _____ as a substitute for the subjunctive.   — infinitive
40. This is especially so in spoken German in the (hypothesis/
    conclusion) clause.   — conclusion

Replace the general subjunctive of the conclusion clause with
würde + *infinitive.*

41. Wenn der Staubsauger nicht so laut wäre, kaufte ich ihn.
    Wenn der Staubsauger nicht so laut wäre, _____ _____
    _____ _____.   — würde ich ihn kaufen

42. Wenn er nicht immer so hungrig wäre, äße er weniger. Wenn
    er nicht immer so hungrig wäre, _____ _____ _____ _____.   — würde er weniger
                                                                                   essen

43. Du gingest zu Fuß, wenn das Benzin viel teurer wäre.
    _____ _____ _____ _____ _____, wenn das Benzin viel
    teurer wäre.   — Du würdest zu Fuß
                                                                                   gehen

44. Wenn Ihnen unser neuer Deodorant Spray nicht gefiele, täte
    es uns sehr leid. Wenn Ihnen unser neuer Deodorant Spray
    nicht gefiele, _____ _____ _____ _____ _____ _____.   — würde es uns sehr
                                                                                   leid tun

Change the **würde**-*clause into a clause using the general subjunctive.*

45. Wenn Sie unsere Hautcreme (skin cream) täglich verwenden,
    würden Sie schöner aussehen. Wenn Sie unsere Hautcreme
    täglich verwenden, _____ _____ _____ _____.   — sähen Sie schöner aus
46. Wenn er nicht lebte, um zu essen, würde er gesünder sein.
    Wenn er nicht lebte, um zu essen, _____ _____ _____.   — wäre er gesünder

3. Time and tense in the subjunctive

47. The statement **Wenn er Geld hätte, ginge er auf Ferien** indicates that if he had money, he would go on vacation (now/ sometime in the future/now or sometime in the future).

— now or sometime in the future

48. When the general subjunctive is used to express conditions that refer to the past, it is formed by combining **hätte** or _____ with the past participle.

— **wäre**

Complete with the proper form of **haben** *or* **sein.**

49. Ich _____ den Job bekommen, wenn ich das Abitur gehabt _____.

— hätte, hätte

50. _____ Sie pünktlich gewesen, Herr Schuster, dann _____ Sie die Stelle bekommen.

— Wären, hätten

51. Ja, Frau Hartwig, wenn ich das gewußt _____, dann _____ ich schneller gefahren.

— hätte, wäre

Restate, changing the present/future time frame to the past time frame of the general subjunctive.

52. Wenn unser Basketball Team besser spielte, würde es das Spiel gewinnen. Wenn unser Basketball Team besser _____ _____, _____ es das Spiel _____.

— gespielt hätte, hätte . . . gewonnen

53. Ich würde Biologie studieren, wenn dieses Fach nicht so schwer wäre. Ich _____ Biologie _____, wenn dieses Fach nicht so schwer _____ _____.

— hätte . . . studiert, gewesen wäre

54. Wenn Norbert das wüßte, würde er gern kommen. Wenn Norbert das _____ _____, _____ er gern _____.

— gewußt hätte, wäre . . . gekommen.

4. Omission of **wenn**

55. When **wenn** is omitted at the beginning of a hypothesis clause, the word order changes to (Verb-Last/Verb-Subject/ Subject-Verb) word order.

— Verb-Subject

56. In the conclusion clause, the words _____ or _____ may or may not be used.

— **so, dann**

Restate, omitting **wenn.**

57. Wenn wir nicht auf dem Mond gelandet wären, dann könnten die Kinder noch glauben, er wäre ein Stück grüner Käse.

_____,

dann könnten die Kinder noch glauben, er wäre ein Stück grüner Käse.

— Wären wir nicht auf dem Mond gelandet,

58. Wenn wir mehr Geld für die Probleme auf der Erde ausgäben, dann gäbe es weniger Slums.

_____

_____,

dann gäbe es weniger Slums.

— Gäben wir mehr Geld für die Probleme auf der Erde aus,

Translate into German.

59. Wären Heinz und Inge nicht so spät gekommen, so hätten sie Gerhard hier getroffen.

_____

_____

— If Heinz and Inge had not come so late, they would have met Gerhard here.

60. Hätte Petra laut um Hilfe gerufen, hätte man sie schneller gefunden.

_____

_____

— If Petra had called loudly for help, one would have found her more quickly.

61. Ich würde schon wieder Fußball spielen, hätte ich
mir nicht das Bein gebrochen.

_____

_____

— I would play soccer
again if I hadn't
broken my leg.

62. Könnte ich Ulrike diese schöne Wohnung zeigen, dann
würde sie vielleicht die Miete nicht zu hoch finden.

_____

_____

— If I could show
Ulrike this nice
apartment, then per-
haps she would find
that the rent is not
too high.

Probe-Test

A. *Translate the underlined expressions.*

1. <u>Schämen Sie sich!</u> _____

2. <u>Keinen Ausweis!</u> _____

3. <u>Ich ginge schnell</u> nach Hause. _____

4. Ich würde so tun, <u>als hätte ich nichts gesehen.</u> _____

5. <u>Sie behielte den Hund.</u> _____

6. <u>Was hätten Sie</u> in dieser Situation <u>getan?</u> _____

7. <u>Ich wäre fortgegangen</u>, um Hilfe zu holen. _____

B. *Complete.*

1. In the subjunctive, weak verbs add _____ between the stem and the ending.

2. The endings of the general subjunctive of weak verbs are the same as those of _____

_____.

3. Strong verbs signal their subjunctive by an _____ on the form of the past tense if

they have the stem vowel _____, _____ or _____.

4. All verbs have _____ endings in the general subjunctive.

5. A substitute for the subjunctive is _____ .

6. The past tense frame of the general subjunctive is formed with _____ and

_____ .

7. When **wenn** is omitted in a hypothesis clause, the word order must be _____ .

C. *Express in German using the general subjunctive.*

1. I wished you were here. _____

2. He acted as if he had money. _____

3. If only I had time! _____

4. I wished I knew everything. _____

D. *Rewrite, putting the verbs into the general subjunctive.*

1. Wenn ich Zeit habe, komme ich zu dir.

_____

2. Wenn es keine Inflation gibt, geht alles besser.

_____

3. Wenn ich zu Hause bin, bin ich glücklich.

_____

4. Es ist gut, wenn Sie mir helfen können.

_____

5. Ich freue mich, wenn ich mitgehen darf.

_____

6. Wenn ich Geld habe, kaufe ich es.

_____

E. *Rewrite, using the* **würde***-construction in the conclusion clause instead of the general subjunctive.*

1. Wenn ich Zeit hätte, flöge ich nach Haus.

   _____

2. Wenn du heute kämest, bliebe ich zu Haus.

   _____

F. *Rewrite, using the general subjunctive instead of the* **würde***-construction.*

1. Wenn Sie es haben möchten, würde ich es Ihnen geben.

   _____

2. Wenn du heute schriebest, würde ich sehr froh sein.

   _____

3. Wenn ihr arm wäret, würdet ihr viele Probleme haben.

   _____

G. *Complete, using the appropriate subjunctive form of the cue verbs in the* **past** *time frame.*

1. Wenn er früher _____ _____, _____
                heiraten   haben   sein

   er glücklicher _____.
                sein

2. Wenn ich pünktlich _____ _____,
                sein   sein

   _____ ich die Stelle _____.
       haben   bekommen

3. Wenn wir mehr _____ _____,
                reisen   sein

   _____ wir mehr von der Welt _____.
       haben   sehen

4. Wenn du mehr _____ _____, dann
                                studieren   haben

_____ du die Antwort _____.
        haben   wissen

H. *Express in German.*

1. If only you had written! _____

2. If only she had had more time. _____

3. If only I had not been sick. _____

I. *Rewrite, omiting* **wenn.**

1. Wenn ich es nur nicht tun müßte! _____

2. Wenn er nur mehr Zeit hätte! _____

3. Wenn er wollte, könnte er es tun. _____

4. Wenn du uns nur geschrieben hättest! _____

J. *Rewrite, putting the cue words into the proper general subjunctive form and word order.*

1. Wenn ich Zeit hätte, (kommen/ich/gerne/zu dir).

_____

2. Wenn das Wetter wärmer wäre, (wir/schwimmen/gehen).

_____

3. Ich hätte es nicht geglaubt, (wenn/gesehen/ich/nicht/habe).

_____

4. (haben/wissen/Ihre Adresse/ich), dann hätte ich Ihnen geschrieben.

_____

5. Ich würde mir ein Auto kaufen, (das Benzin/nicht/wenn/so teuer/sein).

_____

K. *Complete in your own way the "If" wishes below.*

1. Wenn ich viel Geld hätte, _____

_____

2. Wenn ich jetzt nicht in der Klasse sein müßte, _____

_____

3. Wenn ich nicht so dumm gewesen wäre, _____

_____

4. Wenn Deutsch nicht so schwer wäre, _____

_____

5. Wenn _____

_____

L. **Reading comprehension**

Was würden Sie sich wünschen, wenn Ihnen eine gute Fee (fairy) drei Wünsche erfüllte? (Diese Frage steht auf Seite 372 im Lehrbuch.) Hier ist eine kleine Geschichte . . . als Warnung.

Eine gute Fee sagte einmal zu einem armen Mann und zu seiner Frau: ,,Ihr dürft euch drei Dinge wünschen." Der Mann war sehr hungrig und sagte: ,,Liebe Fee, ich wäre sehr glücklich, wenn du mir eine schöne, große, fette Wurst geben würdest." Sofort war die Wurst auf dem Tisch. Seine Frau wurde sehr böse und sagte: ,,Du Dummkopf, du hättest uns Gold wünschen können!" Jetzt wurde der Mann auch böse, denn er wollte seine Wurst essen. Er sagte: ,,Ich würde lieber die Wurst an deiner Nase hängen sehen, als etwas anderes zu wünschen!" Sofort hing die Wurst an der Nase seiner Frau. Sie schimpfte, und jetzt mußte der Mann die Fee bitten, die Wurst wieder wegzunehmen.

So waren alle drei Wünsche erfüllt und die armen Leute waren so arm wie vorher.

Answer in English.

1. Warum ist diese Geschichte eine Warnung? _____

    _____

2. Warum wurde die Frau böse? _____

    _____

3. Was mußte der Mann am Ende wünschen? _____

    _____

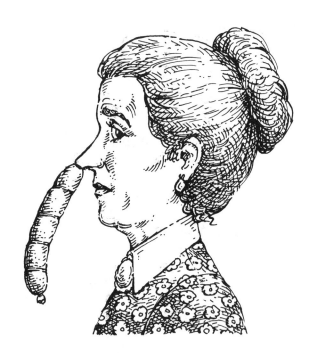

Erweitern Sie Ihren Wortschatz!

A. Englisch-Deutsch

1. bed _____
2. rent _____
3. inflation _____
4. credit card _____
5. fire _____
6. dog _____
7. apartment _____
8. possibility _____
9. manager _____
10. restaurant _____
11. pocket, satchel, purse _____
12. atom _____
13. happy _____

14. to happen _____
15. to keep, retain _____
16. to notify, alarm _____
17. to try _____
18. to break _____
19. to ask _____
20. to go away _____
21. to eat (said of animals) _____
22. to wish _____
23. in love _____
24. Second World War _____
25. to call for help _____
_____

B. Deutsch-Englisch

1. der Konjunktiv _____

2. das Tal _____

3. der Kellner _____

4. der Ausweis _____

5. der Dieb _____

6. das Kernkraftwerk _____

7. die Bergtour _____

8. die Kernspaltung _____

9. die Kernphysik _____

10. die Hypothese _____

11. die Entdeckung _____

12. die Hundemarke _____

13. meinen _____

14. zurücklegen _____

15. holen _____

16. verlieren _____

17. das Uran _____

18. spalten _____

19. leihen _____

20. stecken _____

21. stehenbleiben _____

22. pensioniert _____

23. öfters _____

24. bis ans Ende der Welt _____

25. Schämen Sie sich! _____

_____

NAME _____ KURS _____ DATUM _____

Hör zu . . .und antworte!   Antwortbogen

Übung **A**. *Circle A or B.*

1. A B   2. A B   3. A B   4. A B   5. A B   6. A B

Übung **B**. *Circle* **Richtig** *or* **Falsch**.

1. R F   2. R F   3. R F   4. R F   5. R F   6. R F

7. R F   8. R F

Übung **C**. *Circle A, B, or C. More than one answer may be correct.*

1. A B C   2. A B C   3. A B C   4. A B C

5. A B C   6. A B C   7. A B C   8. A B C

9. A B C   10. A B C   11. A B C   12. A B C

13. A B C   14. A B C   15. A B C   16. A B C

17. A B C   18. A B C   19. A B C   20. A B C

21. A B C   22. A B C

Übung **D**. *Circle A or B.*

1. A   B   2. A   B   3. A   B   4. A   B   5. A   B   6. A   B

7. A   B   8. A   B   9. A   B

Kapitel 16

Selbst-Test

DIALOG

Translate the underlined expressions.

1. <u>Als wenn er</u> auf einer Rennbahn <u>wäre</u>!
2. Sie tut nur so, <u>also ob sie unschuldig wäre</u>.
3. <u>Er sagte, sie sei zu schnell gefahren</u>.

4. <u>Er behauptete, sie habe nicht gestoppt</u>.

5. <u>Er hätte den Unfall verhindern können</u>.

— As if he were
— as if she were
— He said she had driven too fast.
— He claimed that she hadn't stopped.
— He could have prevented the accident.

1. Subjunctive after **als ob** and **als wenn**

6. The conjunctions **als ob** and **als wenn** correspond to English _____.

— *as if*

7. Both expressions require the use of the _____ or _____ plus the infinitive.

— general subjunctive, **würde**

8. Both expressions cause (V-L/V-S) word order.

— V-L

9. When the event reported took place prior to the time when it is reported, the (past/present) subjunctive is generally used.

— past

10. When the event reported implies a future event, the _____-construction is used.

— **würde**

Complete, putting the cue clause into the appropriate time frame of the general subjunctive.

11. (er ist heute krank) Er sieht aus, als ob _____.

— er heute krank wäre

12. (er ist gestern krank gewesen) Er sieht aus, als ob _____.

— er gestern krank gewesen wäre

13. (er ist krank gewesen) Er sah gestern aus, als ob _____.

    — er krank gewesen wäre

14. (er hat den Unfall gesehen) Er antwortete, als ob _____.

    — er den Unfall gesehen hätte

15. (er sieht Fräulein Lechner nicht) Vor Gericht tut er, als ob _____.

    — er Fräulein Lechner nicht sähe

16. (Du hast ihn gern wiedergesehen), Es scheint mir, als ob _____.

    — du ihn gern wiedergesehen hättest.

17. (sie weiß die Antwort) Sie tat, als ob _____.

    — sie die Antwort wüßte

Complete, using the cue phrase in a **würde**-*construction.*

18. (ein Unfall passiert) Es sah aus, als ob _____.

    — ein Unfall passieren würde

19. (er gewinnt den Fall) Es schien, als ob _____.

    — er den Fall gewinnen würde

20. When **ob** is omitted from the phrase **als ob**, the verb (follows immediately after **ob**/stands at the end of the clause).

    — follows immediately after **ob**

Translate **als**.

21. Der Dieb tat, als schämte er sich. _____
22. Er rief die Polizei, als er den Dieb sah. _____
23. Viele Diebe haben mehr Geld als Leute, die arbeiten. _____
24. Als wüßte ich das nicht! _____

    — *as if*
    — *when*
    — *than*
    — *As if*

2. Subjunctive in indirect statements

25. The subjunctive is used not only in wishes and unreal situations, but also in _____ statements.

    — indirect

26. A direct quotation uses the indicative and is set off by _____ _____.

    — quotation marks

Rewrite the English indirect statement in direct discourse.

27. He asserted that he was not guilty.

_____

    — He asserted: "I am not guilty."

28. The verb in the introductory phrase of an indirect statement in German may be in either the (present or past/ present or future) tense.

— present or past

Report the direct quotations as indirect statements.

29. Er sagt: „Ich habe keine Zeit." Er sagt, _____ _____ keine Zeit.

— er hätte

30. Er sagte: „Ich habe kein Geld." Er sagte, _____ _____ kein Geld.

— er hätte

31. Er sagt: „Ich habe gestern kein Glück gehabt." Er sagt, _____ _____ gestern kein Glück _____.

— er hätte, gehabt

32. Er hat gesagt: „Ich werde morgen die Rechnung bezahlen." Er hat gesagt, _____ _____ morgen die Rechnung _____.

— er würde, bezahlen

33. Sie schreibt: „Ich gebe zu viel Geld aus." Sie schreibt, _____ _____ zu viel Geld _____.

— sie gäbe, aus

34. Gestern schrieb sie uns: „Ich komme bald nach Haus." Gestern schrieb sie uns, _____ _____ bald nach Haus.

— sie käme

35. Sie hat uns geschrieben: „Ich heirate im Juni." Sie hat uns geschrieben, _____ _____ im Juni _____.

— sie würde, heiraten

3. Subjunctive in indirect questions

36. The general subjunctive is used not only in indirect statements, but also in indirect _____.

— questions

37. An indirect question begins with either **ob** or a _____ word.

— question

Restate as indirect questions.

38. „Wer ist das junge Mädchen?" Sie fragte, _____.

— wer das junge Mädchen wäre

39. „Haben Sie heute Zeit?" Er wollte wissen, _____.

— ob ich heute Zeit hätte

40. „Wann hast du Zeit?" Er fragte mich, _____.

— wann ich Zeit hätte

41. „Wo wohnt sie?" Sie fragte, _____.

— wo sie wohnte

42. „Wann fängt das Semester an?" Sie wollten wissen, _____.

— wann das Semester anfinge

4. Subjunctive in indirect commands with **sollen**

43. Indirect commands are expressed in German with the subjunctive of the modal _____ plus the _____ of the main verb.

— **sollen**, infinitive

Restate as indirect commands.

44. „Rufen Sie mich heute an!"
    Er sagte, _____.

— ich sollte ihn heute anrufen

45. „Kommen Sie bald, Herr und Frau Eisenhauer!"
    Sie sagten, _____.

— wir sollten bald kommen

46. „Schick mir bald das Geld!"
    Ich schrieb meinem Vater, _____.

— er sollte mir bald das Geld schicken

5. Subjunctive of politeness

Change the request into a more polite form by using the subjunctive.

47. Haben Sie noch etwas Zeit? _____ noch etwas Zeit?
48. Werden Sie mir helfen? _____ mir helfen, bitte?
49. Darf ich Sie um etwas bitten? _____ Sie um etwas bitten?
50. Kannst du mir zehn Mark schicken? _____ mir zehn Mark schicken?

— Hätten Sie
— Würden Sie
— Dürfte ich

— Könntest du

Complete in German.

51. *Be so good as to help me.* (less polite)

    _____, und helfen Sie

    mir.

— Sind Sie so gut

52. *Would you be so good as to help me?* (very polite)

    _____, mir zu helfen?

— Wären (*or* Seien) Sie so gut

53. *Do you have a cigarette?* (less polite)

    _____ eine Zigarette?

— Haben Sie

54. *Would you have a cigarette?* (very polite)

    _____ eine Zigarette?

— Hätten Sie

6. The special subjunctive

55. The special subjunctive is an alternate form to the general
    subjunctive and is used primarily in _____ _____. — indirect statements
56. It is (frequently/rarely) used in spoken German. — rarely
57. Is there a difference in meaning between the general
    subjunctive and the special subjunctive? (Yes/No) — No
58. The general subjunctive is derived from the (infinitive/
    past tense). — past tense
59. The special subjunctive is derived from the (infinitive/
    past participle). — infinitive
60. The personal endings of the special subjunctive are (the
    same as/different from) those of the general subjunctive. — the same as
61. Strong verbs (do/do not) umlaut in the special subjunctive. — do not
62. The special subjunctive is usually not used when its forms
    are identical to those of the _____ tense indicative. — present
63. In spoken German, the special subjunctive is used primarily
    in the third person (singular/plural). — singular
64. In the third person singular, the present tense indicative
    ends in _____, but the special subjunctive ends in _____. — -t, -e
65. The special subjunctive can also be used in all forms of the
    singular of the modals _____, _____, and _____, and the
    verb _____. — **dürfen, können,
                      müssen, wissen**
66. It can be used with these four verbs because its forms are
    clearly different from those of the _____ _____ indicative. — present tense

Restate, using the special subjunctive.

67. Sie sagte, sie hätte Zeit.

    Sie sagte, _____. — sie habe Zeit

68. Arthur sagte, er ginge heute nach Hause.

    Arthur sagte, _____. — er gehe heute nach
                                                       Haus

69. Er fragte mich, ob ich es wüßte.

    Er fragte mich, _____. — ob ich es wisse

70. Er schrieb, daß er Rock und Roll gern hörte.

    Er schrieb, daß _____. — er Rock und Roll gern
                                                       höre

Restate, changing the direct quotation into an indirect statement.
If the special subjunctive form is not clearly distinct from the
indicative form in the cue sentence, use the general subjunctive.

71. Er schreibt: „Sie kommen morgen."
    Er schreibt, sie _____ morgen.   — kämen
72. Er schreibt: „Sie kommt morgen."
    Er schreibt, sie _____ morgen.   — komme (*or* käme)
73. Er schreibt: „Du weißt die Adresse."
    Er schreibt, du _____ die Adresse.   — wissest (*or* wüßtest)
74. Er fragt mich: „Wissen Sie die Adresse?"
    Er fragt mich, ob ich die Adresse _____.   — wisse (*or* wüßte)

Complete, putting the cue verb into the general subjunctive, the
special subjunctive, or both if appropriate.

75. (haben)   Er sagte, sie _____ kein Geld.   — habe (*or* hätte)
76. (dürfen) Ich fragte, ob ich rauchen _____.   — dürfe (*or* dürfte)
77. (geben)   Sie wollten wissen, ob es hier einen Job _____.   — gebe (*or* gäbe)
78. (werden) Sie schreiben, daß sie bald kommen _____.   — würden
79. (werden) Sie sagte, daß sie bald schreiben _____.   — werde (*or* würde)
80. (haben)   Er sagte, daß wir noch viel Zeit _____.   — hätten

The special subjunctive of **sein**

81. The special subjunctive of **sein** can be used in (the singular/
    the plural/both the singular and the plural).   — both the singular and
                                                                   the plural

Complete, using both the special subjunctive and the general
subjunctive of **sein.**

82. Er wollte wissen, ob ich heute zu Hause _____ (*or* _____).   — sei, wäre
83. Sie sagte, du _____ (*or* _____) heute zu Hause.   — seist, wärest
84. Wir schrieben ihm, er _____ (*or* _____) immer willkommen.   — sei, wäre
85. Er schrieb ihr, sie _____ (*or* _____) willkommen.   — sei, wäre
86. Ich behauptete, es _____ (*or* _____) nicht recht, das zu tun.   — sei, wäre
87. Sie tat, als ob wir nicht hier _____ (*or* _____).   — seien, wären
88. Es schien, als ob ihr heute nicht zu Hause _____ (*or* _____).   — seiet, wäret
89. Ich möchte wissen, ob Sie heute zu Hause _____
    (*or* _____).   — seien, wären
90. Er wollte wissen, ob Sie Amerikaner _____ (*or* _____).   — seien, wären

91. The past time frame of the special subjunctive is formed like
    that of the general subjunctive, except that the auxiliary
    _____ or _____ replaces **wäre** or **hätte**.   — **sei, habe**

Complete, using the special subjunctive.

92. Er sagte, er wäre gestern zu Haus gewesen. Er sagte, er
    _____ gestern zu Haus _____.   — sei . . . gewesen

93. Der Richter fragte sie, ob sie das Rotlicht gesehen hätte. Der
    Richter fragte sie, ob sie das Rotlicht _____ _____.   — gesehen habe

94. Ich fragte ihn, wer das getan hätte. Ich fragte ihn, wer das

    _____ _____.   — getan habe

95. Wir möchten wissen, ob er morgen zu Haus wäre. Wir
    möchten wissen, ob er morgen zu Haus _____   — sei

Probe-Test

A. *Translate the underlined expressions.*

1. Sie tat, <u>als habe sie nichts gehört</u>. _____

2. Er tat, <u>als sei ich immer willkommen</u>. _____

3. Sie schrieb, <u>daß es keinen Religionsunterricht gebe</u>. _____

4. Er sagte, <u>man dürfe den Rasen nicht betreten</u>. _____

   _____

5. Ich fragte, <u>ob noch ein Platz frei sei</u>. _____

B. *Rewrite the clause. If it contains* **als ob**, *change it to* **als**, *and vice versa.*

1. Es sieht aus, als ob er sein Geld verloren hätte. Es sieht aus, _____

   _____

2. Er tut, als wollte er die Rechnung bezahlen. Er tut, _____

   _____

3. Es schien, als ob der Kellner die Polizei rufen würde. Es schien, _____

   _____

C. *Complete.*

1. The general subjunctive is derived from _____.

2. The special subjunctive is derived from _____.

3. The special subjunctive is used especially in _____.

4. When the **ob** is omitted in the phrase **als ob**, the word order changes from

   _____ to _____.

5. The special subjunctive is used only when it is not identical with _____

   _____.

D. *Complete, changing the direct quotation into an indirect statement.*

1. ,,*Vor Sonnenaufgang* ist ein vieldiskutiertes Stück."

   In der Zeitung steht, daß _____

2. ,,Hier sind wir ungestört."

   Helene sagte, hier _____

3. ,,Wie heißt du?"

   Loth fragte mich, wie _____

4. ,,Darf ich ,du' zu dir sagen?"

   Er fragte mich, ob _____

5. ,,Liebst du mich"?

   Ich fragte ihn/sie, ob _____

E. *Complete with the German equivalent. Use the general subjunctive or the special subjunctive, whichever is appropriate. If both are possible, put the second form in parentheses.*

1. *They said they had no time.*

   Sie sagten, sie _____

2. *She said she had no time.*

   Sie sagte, _____

3. *He said he couldn't do that.*

   Er sagte, _____

4. *I would never do that.*

   Ich _____

5. *Would you help me, please?*

   _____ , bitte?

6. *We answered that we were at home.*

   Wir antworteten, wir _____

7. *He answered he was at home.*

   Er antwortete, er _____

8. *It looks as if you* (formal) *were coming.*

   Es sieht aus, als _____

9. *It seems that I may do this.*

   Es scheint, daß ich das _____

10. *He acts as if he knew everything.*

    Er tut, als ob er alles _____

11. *You said there was no pharmacy here.*

    Sie haben gesagt, _____ keine Apotheke hier.

12. *He said that I ought to write.* (use **müssen**)

    Er sagte, daß ich _____

13. *Could you give me a cigarette, please?*

   _____ mir bitte eine Zigarette geben?

14. *They wrote that you could come.*

   Sie schrieben, daß du _____

15. *The police said I should drive more slowly.*

   Die Polizei hat gesagt, ich _____

16, *He said I spoke German well.*

   Er meinte, ich _____ gut Deutsch.

17. *Would you* (familiar) *have time tomorrow?*

   _____ morgen Zeit?

F. *Translate into English.*

   1. Er hat gesagt, er kenne kein besseres Fahrrad.

   _____

   2. Er wollte wissen, wie lange ich verheiratet sei.

   _____

   3. Er sagte, wir sollten zusammen ein Bier trinken.

   _____

   4. Auf dem Schild stand, hier sei alles verboten.

   _____

   5. Er fragte mich, warum ich so schnell gefahren wäre.

   _____

   6. Ich dachte, es wäre möglich. _____

7. Es lebe der König! _____

8. Es werde Licht! _____

G. *Change the direct quotation into an indirect statement. Use the special subjunctive. Maintain the same tense.*

1. „Fritz ist nach Berlin gefahren."

   Er sagte, Fritz _____

2. „Meine Mutter ist in Freiburg."

   Sie sagte, ihre Mutter _____

3. „Ich habe die Adresse gefunden."

   Er sagte, _____

4. „Sie hat die Adresse."

   Er sagte, _____

5. „Bist du krank gewesen?"

   Sie fragte, ob _____

6. „Sind Sie krank?"

   Der Arzt fragte, ob _____

H. *On the basis of your own knowledge or experience of differences between American and German culture, write an essay describing them in 50 words or less. Here are three examples. In the first two, you are an American. In the third, you are a German. (If you have had no "culture shock" experiences, translate both examples.)*

1. Ich war in Göttingen. Ich wollte einen Freund im zweiten Stock[1] besuchen. Als ich im zweiten Stock ankam, stand auf einem Schild „Erster Stock". Da sagte man mir, daß in Deutschland der zweite Stock der erste Stock sei. Der „erste" Stock hieße „Erdgeschoß".

---

[1]Another common expression for **der Stock** is **die Etage**.

2. Ich kam in mein erstes deutsches Hotel. Ich fragte: ,,Wo ist die Toilette? ''
Der Hotelportier sagte mir, ich solle zur Tür geradeaus mit dem Schild
"OO" [Null Null] gehen. Das sei das ,,W.C.''

3. Ich war zu Besuch in Kansas City. Ich wohnte im Hilton Hotel. Als ich im Lift
war, sah ich, daß es keinen 13. Stock gibt. Als ich fragte warum, sagte man mir,
dreizehn sei eine Unglückszahl. Es gäbe auch kein Zimmer Nummer 13.

_____

_____

_____

_____

_____

_____

_____

_____

I. *You are Frau Dr. Ilse von Unterberg. You are hosting American exchange students in your villa in Regensburg. One of the students asks: ,,Warum tragen Sie einen goldenen Ring an der rechten Hand?'' You are delighted about the question. Can you explain the German custom?*

The following words and expressions may be helpful.

während man verlobt ist	*while one is engaged*
an der linken Hand	*on the left hand*
wenn man dann verheiratet ist	*when one gets married*

_____

_____

_____

Erweitern Sie Ihren Wortschatz!

A. Englisch-Deutsch

1. accident _____

2. driver's license _____

3. court _____

4. police _____

5. report _____

6. car driver _____

7. lawn _____

8. nonsense, "bull" _____

9. judge _____

10. intersection _____

11. red light (*traffic*) _____

12. to take a walk _____

13. to sit down _____

14. to stop _____

15. to prevent _____

16. to claim, assert _____

17. to close, shut _____

18. to warn _____

19. alleged(ly) _____

20. slow(ly) _____

21. innocent _____

22. at most _____

23. unpleasant _____

24. to act like, to do as if _____

25. to be welcome _____

B. Deutsch-Englisch

1. der Fall _____

2. die Gasse _____

3. der Angeklagte _____

4. der Zeuge _____

5. der Verkehrsunfall _____

6. die Geschwindigkeitsbegrenzung _____

_____

7. die Fahrschule _____

8. das Kleid _____

9. die Rennbahn _____

10. der Religionsunterricht _____

11. die Behauptung _____

12. das Kompliment _____

13. beachten _____

14. betreten _____

15. anfahren _____

16. hängen _____

17. losfahren _____

18. nicht lang genug _____

19. rein _____

20. schuldig _____

21. überrascht _____

22. möglich _____

23. innerhalb _____

24. gerade _____

25. Das ist doch reiner Quatsch! _____

_____

Hör zu . . .und antworte!   Antwortbogen

Übung **A**. *Circle* **Richtig** *or* **Falsch**.

1. R F	2. R F	3. R F	4. R F	5. R F	6. R F
7. R F	8. R F	9. R F	10. R F	11. R F	12. R F
13. R F	14. R F	15. R F	16. R F	17. R F	18. R F
19. R F	20. R F				

Übung **B**. *Circle A, B, or C.*

1. A B C	2. A B C	3. A B C	4. A B C
5. A B C	6. A B C	7. A B C	8. A B C

Übung **C**. *Circle* **Deutsch** *or* **Amerikanisch**.

1. D A	2. D A	3. D A	4. D A	5. D A	6. D A
7. D A	8. D A	9. D A	10. D A	11. D A	12. D A

Übung **D.** *Circle* **Richtig** *or* **Falsch**.

1. R F   2. R F   3. R F   4. R F   5. R F   6. R F

7. R F   8. R F   9. R F   10. R F   11. R F   12. R F

13. R F   14. R F   15. R F   16. R F   17. R F   18. R F

19. R F   20. R F   21. R F   22. R F   23. R F   24. R F

25. R F   26. R F   27. R F   28. R F   29. R F   30. R F

Übung **E.** *Complete each question with one word.*

1. _____ 2. _____ 3. _____ 4. _____

Kapitel 17

Selbst-Test

DIALOG

Translate the underlined expressions.

1. Im Witz darf vieles gesagt werden.
   — In jokes many things may be said.

2. Wollen Sie schon gehen?
   — Do you want to leave already?

3. In der Schweiz werden vier Sprachen gesprochen.
   — Four languages are spoken

4. Der Witz wird zur unblutigen Revolution.
   — The joke becomes

5. Viele Witze wurden heimlich erzählt.
   — were told

6. Er ist verhaftet worden.
   — He was (has been) arrested.

1. The passive voice

7. The active voice and the passive voice express (the same/ different) meanings.
   — the same

Are the following statements in the active voice or the passive voice?

8. The police arrest the criminal. _____
   — active
9. The criminal is arrested by the police. _____
   — passive
10. Die Polizei verhaftet den Verbrecher. _____
    — active
11. Der Verbrecher wird von der Polizei verhaftet. _____
    — passive

12. In English the passive voice is formed by using the verb _____ with the _____ _____ of the main verb.
    — *to be*, past participle

13. The agent is cited in a prepositional phrase with _____.
    — *by*

14. In German the verb corresponding to English *to be* as the auxiliary in the passive voice is _____. — **werden**
15. In German the preposition used is _____. — **von**
16. In addition to the auxiliary and the preposition, the third element of the passive construction in both German and English is the _____ _____. — past participle

Give the three elements that constitute the passive voice in these statements.

17. Die Reklame wird von vielen Leuten gelesen. — wird/von/gelesen
18. Ist es wahr, daß viele Planeten von Astronauten erforscht werden? — von/erforscht/werden

19. In a main clause, the element of the passive voice that stands last is the _____ _____. — past participle
20. In a dependent clause, the last element is the _____ _____. — conjugated verb
21. The preposition **von** introduces the (agent/object). — agent
22. The preposition **von**, used to introduce the agent, requires that the _____ case be used. — dative
23. The agent (is always/may not always be) expressed. — may not always be

Restate, omitting the agent.

24. Das Buch wird von mir gekauft. _____ _____ _____ _____ — Das Buch wird gekauft.

Restate, adding the cue agent.

25. (der Professor) Die Studenten werden gefragt. Die Studenten _____ _____ _____ _____ _____. — werden von dem Professor gefragt

26. In the passive voice, (the past participle/**werden**) changes its form according to person. — **werden**

*Supply the proper form of **werden**.*

27. Du _____ heute eingeladen. (*You are invited today*) — wirst
28. Wann _____ Sie eingeladen? — werden
29. Ich _____ oft eingeladen. — werde
30. Wann _____ ihr eingeladen? — werdet
31. Warum _____ sie nicht eingeladen? — wird (*or* werden)

Complete the passive statements.

32. Die Sekretärin ruft Herrn Schuster ins Büro.
    Herr Schuster _____ von _____ ins Büro _____.

    — wird, der Sekretärin, gerufen

33. Frau Hartwig fragt ihn über seinen Lebenslauf.
    Er _____ von _____ über seinen Lebenslauf _____.

    — wird, Frau Hartwig, gefragt

34. Sie stellt ihm viele Fragen.
    Viele Fragen _____ ihm von _____ _____.

    — werden, ihr gestellt

35. Er beantwortet alle Fragen.
    Alle Fragen _____ von _____ _____.

    — werden, ihm beantwortet

Answer the question using the passive voice.

36. Von wem wird Herr Schuster interviewt?   (Frau Hartwig)
    Herr Schuster _____ _____ _____ _____ _____.

    — wird von Frau Hartwig interviewt

37. Von wem werden die Abiturienten geprüft (*examined*)?
    (die Professoren)
    Die Abiturienten _____ _____ _____ _____ _____.

    — werden von den Professoren geprüft

Restate, using the passive voice.

38. Ich bezahle die Rechnung.

    _____

    — Die Rechnung wird von mir bezahlt.

39. Wir gewinnen das Basketballspiel.

    _____

    — Das Basketballspiel wird von uns gewonnen.

40. Die Biologielehrerin beeinflußt dich.

    _____

    _____

    — Du wirst von der Biologielehrerin beeinflußt.

41. Die Baufirma braucht viele Arbeiter.

_____

_____

— Viele Arbeiter werden von der Baufirma gebraucht.

2. Tenses in the passive voice

42. The passive voice is used in (some/all) tenses.
43. In the past passive, **werden** becomes _____.
44. In the present perfect and past perfect passive, **werden** becomes _____.
45. In the future passive, **werden** (changes/does not change).
46. In all the tenses, the past participle (changes/stays the same).

— all
— **wurden**

— **worden**
— does not change

— stays the same

Supply the correct form of **werden** *in the tense indicated.*

47. (*present*) Mein Lebenslauf _____ gelesen.
48. (*past*) Mein Lebenslauf _____ gelesen.
49. (*present perfect*) Mein Lebenslauf ist gelesen _____.
50. (*past perfect*) Mein Lebenslauf war gelesen _____.
51. (*future*) Mein Lebenslauf wird gelesen _____.

— wird
— wurde
— worden
— worden
— werden

Complete the passive statement in the tense indicated. Use the verb **vorschlagen** *to suggest.*

52. (*present*) Ein paar Verbesserungen _____ von dem Professor _____.
53. (*past*) Ein paar Verbesserungen _____ von dem Professor _____.
54. (*present perfect*) Ein paar Verbesserungen _____ von dem Professor _____ _____.
55. (*past perfect*) Ein paar Verbesserungen _____ von dem Professor _____ _____.
56. (*future*) Ein paar Verbesserungen _____ von dem Professor vorgeschlagen _____.

— werden, vorgeschlagen

— wurden, vorgeschlagen
— sind, vorgeschlagen, worden

— waren, vorgeschlagen, worden
— werden, werden

Complete in the tense indicated.

57. Die Raumfahrt wird von uns weiter entwickelt.
(*present perfect*) Die Raumfahrt _____ von uns _____ _____.
58. Durch die Mondlandung sind große Fortschritte gemacht worden.
(*past perfect*) Durch die Mondlandung _____ große Fortschritte _____ _____.

— ist, entwickelt worden

— waren, gemacht worden

59. Neue Planeten sind entdeckt worden.
    (*future*) Neue Planeten _____ _____ _____.

— werden entdeckt
werden

Complete the German equivalent.

60. *It's getting serious.* Es _____ ernst.
61. *It will soon become serious.* Es _____ bald ernst _____.
62. *I will do the job.* Ich _____ die Arbeit machen.
63. *The job is being done by me.* Die Arbeit _____ _____
    _____ _____.

64. *He is being called on the phone.* Er _____ _____.

65. When the agent is not a person, **von** is replaced by _____
    or _____.

— wird
— wird, werden
— werde

— wird von mir
gemacht
— wird angerufen

— durch, mit

Supply **von, durch** *or* **mit** *to indicate the ''agent.''*

66. Der Brief wurde _____ der Schreibmaschine geschrieben.
67. Der Brief wurde _____ einem Amerikaner geschrieben.
68. Der Brief wurde _____ seine Forschung entdeckt.

— mit
— von
— durch

3. **man** as a substitute for the passive

69. The **man**-construction (expresses/does not express) the same
    meaning as the passive construction.

— expresses

Give the English equivalents.

70. Hier wird Deutsch gesprochen. _____

71. Man spricht hier Deutsch. _____

— *German is spoken
here.*
— *One speaks German
here.*

Restate the passive statements, using a **man**-*construction or vice
versa.*

72. Viel Zeit wurde verloren.

    _____

— Man verlor viel Zeit.

73. Ein neues Buch wird veröffentlicht (*published*).

    _____

— Man veröffentlicht
ein neues Buch.

74. Man repariert das Auto.

_____ — Das Auto wird
repariert.

75. Man hat ein neues Haus gebaut.

_____ — Ein neues Haus ist
gebaut worden.

4. The passive with modals

76. The passive with a modal auxiliary consists of the modal
plus the _____ _____ plus the infinitive _____. — past participle,
werden

77. In this construction, (the modal/**werden**) changes according
to person and tense. — the modal

Supply the missing elements suggested by the context.

78. Die Rakete muß sofort gebaut _____. — werden
79. Die Raketen _____ sofort gebaut werden. — müssen
80. Keine Raketen dürfen _____ _____. — gebaut werden
81. Nach dem Krieg _____ keine Raketen _____ werden. — durften, gebaut

_Rewrite the sentence using the cue modal. Use the appropriate
person and tense._

82. Mit dieser Rakete wird nicht experimentiert.

(dürfen) _____

_____ — Mit dieser Rakete
darf nicht experi-
mentiert werden.

83. Von Braun wurde nicht von den Russen gefangen.

(wollen) _____

_____ — Von Braun wollte
nicht von den
Russen gefangen
werden.

84. Eine neue Rakete wird entwickelt.

    (sollen) _____

    _____

    — Eine neue Rakete soll entwickelt werden.

85. Diese Raketen werden nicht gebaut.

    (können) Man weiß, daß _____

    _____

    — diese Raketen nicht gebaut werden können.

86. Alle Raketen sind zerstört worden.

    (müssen) _____

    _____

    — Alle Raketen mußten zerstört werden.

87. Diese Frage wurde nicht beantwortet.

    (können) _____

    _____

    — Diese Frage konnte nicht beantwortet werden.

88. Dieses Dilemma wird gelöst werden.

    (können) _____

    _____

    — Dieses Dilemma kann gelöst werden.

5. ein-words and der-words as pronouns

89. Any ein-word or der-word may be used to replace a (noun/verb).

    — noun

90. When used as pronouns, ein-words and der-words have (primary/no) endings.

    — primary

Complete the German equivalent with the appropriate pronoun.

91. *Is this your book? Yes, it is mine.*
    Ist das Ihr Buch? Ja, es ist _____. — meins (*or* meines)

92. *I have a car. When will you buy one too?*
    Ich habe ein Auto. Wann kaufst du auch _____? — eins (*or* eines)

93. *Do you have money? I have none.*
    Haben Sie Geld? Ich habe _____. — keins (*or* keines)

94. *This is my umbrella. Whose is this one?*
    Dies *or* das ist mein Regenschirm. Wem gehört _____? — dieser

95. *I know (this girl/this boy). Which one do you know?*
    Ich kenne (dieses Mädchen/diesen Jungen). _____.Kennst du? — Welches/Welchen

96. *Is this my seat or yours?*
    Ist das mein Platz oder _____? — Ihrer (*or* deiner *or* eurer)

97. *Can I use your car? Ours is broken.*
    Kann ich Ihren Wagen benutzen? _____ ist kaputt. — Unsrer (*or* Unserer)

The following items are based on the Lesestück from Chapter 17. Select the correct word in each sentence.

98. Österreich will eine (Großmacht/Brücke/Hauptstadt) sein. — Brücke

99. Liechtenstein wird noch heute von einem (Kanton/ Politiker/Fürsten) regiert. — Fürsten

100. Während der Hitlerzeit waren alle Österreicher (deutsche Staatsbürger/österreichische Staatsbürger/ohne Staatsbürgerschaft). — deutsche Staatsbürger

101. Nach dem Zweiten Weltkrieg wurde Österreich (annektiert/mobilisiert/befreit). — befreit

102. Im Kanton Graubünden spricht man (Französisch/ Rätoromanisch/Italienisch). — Rätoromanisch

103. Die Schönheit der Schweiz bringt Millionen von (Rohstoffen/ Soldaten/Touristen) ins Land. — Touristen

104. In Liechtenstein werden (wenig/keine/viel) Steuern verlangt. — wenig

Probe-Test

A. *Translate the underlined expressions.*

1. <u>Seit 1924 wird</u> in Liechtenstein mit Schweizer Franken <u>bezahlt</u>.

   _____

2. Viele Leute <u>möchten Staatsbürger von Liechtenstein werden</u>. _____

3. Nach dem Zweiten Weltkrieg <u>wurde Österreich wieder ein unabhängiges Land</u>. _____

   _____

4. Deutsch <u>wird</u> in 22 Kantonen <u>gesprochen</u>. _____

5. <u>Österreich bekam einen neuen Namen</u>. _____

   _____

6. Die Wehrpflicht <u>ist schon immer</u> von den Schweizern <u>ernst genommen worden</u>. _____

   _____

7. „Glücklich ist, wer vergißt, <u>was nicht mehr zu ändern ist</u>." _____

   _____

8. Österreich <u>will eine Brücke</u> zwischen dem Osten und dem Westen <u>sein</u>. _____

   _____

B. *Complete.*

1. The passive voice is formed by combining _____

_____ .

2. The three prepositions that may be the equivalent of English *by* in the passive are _____ ,

_____ , and _____ .

3. The present perfect and past perfect of the passive voice are formed by combining the present or

past tense of _____ plus _____

plus _____ .

4. The future passive is formed by combining _____

_____ .

5. A substitute for the passive is the _____ construction.

6. In a passive construction with a modal, the modal changes according to _____ and

_____ .

C. *Express in German.*

1. The letter was written by hand. _____

2. The house was built by my parents. _____

3. I am being interviewed by a reporter. _____

4. The job is being done by me. _____

5. The job was done by her. _____

6. The job has been done by us. _____

7. I am often called (on the phone). _____

8. I will call you often. _____

9. Austria was annexed by Hitler. _____

D. *Rewrite, using* **man** *as substitute for the passive.*

1. Diese Frage wird nie beantwortet. _____

2. Die Autos werden heute verkauft. _____

E. *Translate into English.*

1. Man wird das Haus bald verkaufen. _____

2. Das Haus wird bald gekauft. _____

_____

F. *Write a sentence and a question, putting the elements into the proper word order. (A double slash indicates a separate clause.)*

1. /weiß/nicht/ich/wann/,,Das Kapital''/Karl Marx/von/wurde/veröffentlicht

_____

2. wissen/Sie//war/das Buch/zum ersten Mal/veröffentlicht/worden/wann/?

_____

G. *Rewrite, using the passive voice.*

1. Der Reporter interviewt mich. _____

2. Man verhaftet ihn. _____

3. Man hat das Haus schon verkauft. _____

4. Wird man das Haus bald verkaufen? _____

H. *Complete with the German equivalent of the English cue.*

1. Hier ist mein Mantel. Wo ist _____?
   yours (familiar)

2. Ist das mein Platz oder _____?
   yours (formal)

3. Hast du Geld? Ich habe _____.
   none

4. Wir sprechen nicht von dem Auto hier, sondern von _____ dort.
   this one

5. Ich wohne bei Familie Schmidt. Bei _____ wohnen Sie?
   which one

6. Haben Sie einen Bleistift? Ich habe _____ vergessen.
   mine

7. Karl Kraus ist mein Kandidat als Präsident. Für _____ bist du?
   which one

I. *Complete with the correct form of the cue pronoun.*

1. (dein-) Ich hab' meine Fahrkarte, aber wo ist denn _____?

2. (dies-) Wir haben unseren Koffer, aber wem gehört denn _____?

3. (Ihr-) Das ist meine Telefonnummer, und was ist denn _____?

4. (dein-) Ich verkaufe meinen Mercedes, und was machst du mit _____?

5. (kein-) Ich habe kein Geld, und er hat auch _____.

6. (unser-) Das hier ist Ihr Platz, und der hier ist _____!

7. (ihr-, *hers*) Mein Freund heißt Bubi, und wie heißt _____?

J. **Reading comprehension**

Read the following passage and then answer the questions in English. Incorporate elements from the question in your answer to show that you have understood the question.

Viele Ausländer (*foreigners*) verstehen das Wort „Hochdeutsch" falsch. Das Wort „hoch" in „Hochdeutsch" bedeutet das Deutsch, das man in dem Teil

Deutschlands sprach, wo das Land „hoch" ist, also im Süden, wo es hohe
Berge gibt. Der Norden ist das Tief- oder Niederland (*lowlands*). Dort sprach
man „Niederdeutsch", auch „Plattdeutsch" genannt. Die Sprache des Südens
wurde später zur Standardsprache für ganz Deutschland. Heute bedeutet
„Hochdeutsch" die deutsche Schriftsprache im Gegensatz (*contrast*) zu den
Dialekten, wie zum Beispiel Bayrisch, Sächsisch, Plattdeutsch, Schwäbisch,
usw.

1. Wie verstehen viele Ausländer das Wort „Hochdeutsch"? _____

   _____

2. Wie ist das Land im Süden Deutschlands? _____

   _____

3. Warum heißt die Sprache im Norden „Niederdeutsch"? _____

   _____

4. Welche Sprache wurde zur Standardsprache? _____

   _____

5. Was bedeutet „Hochdeutsch" heute? _____

   _____

K. *A type of joke that is making the rounds in Germany are the* **Häschen-Witze** (Bunny-Jokes). *A little
bunny always asks* **Hattu** (*instead of* **Hast du**), *gets a straightforward answer, and then draws a stupid
conclusion. Try to translate the following three jokes.*

1. Häschen kommt zum Autogeschäft.
   „Hattu Jaguar?"
   „Wir haben gerade einen bekommen."
   „Muttu aber gut gefangen halten."

   _____

   _____

   _____

   _____

2. Häschen ist auf der Post.
   „Bittu (Bist du) Beamter?"
   „Ja."
   „Hattu Arbeit? "
   „Ja."
   „Dann bittu kein Beamter."

   _____

   _____

   _____

   _____

   _____

3. Häschen kommt in ein Tiergeschäft.
   „Hattu Kater?"
   „Ja, natürlich."
   „Muttu (Du mußt) nicht so viel trinken."

   _____

   _____

   _____

   _____

L. Ich möchte gern wissen . . .

You are asking questions about the German-speaking countries. Use either the passive voice or one of the substitute constructions that you have learned. Below are some noun and verb cues. You provide the other necessary elements. Write out your questions on a separate piece of paper and hand it in to your instructor.

Österreich

das Dirndl/das Reich/die Situation/ das Wienerschnitzel/die Musik/die Wissenschaft/die Aufgabe/
die Bedeutung/tragen/zerschlagen/annektieren/ernst nehmen/ assoziieren/leisten/

Die Schweiz

die Sprache/das Schweizerdeutsch/der Brief/die Zeitung/die Währung/die Uhr/die Arbeit/die
Zukunft/die Frage/sprechen/verstehen/schreiben/eine Frage stellen/zahlen/nennen/exportieren/
leisten/bauen/beantworten/

Liechtenstein

die Armee/das Fürstentum/das Geld/die Staatsbürgerschaft/der Lebensstandard/die Steuer/die
Briefmarke/die Kapitalgesellschaft/abschaffen/brauchen/anschließen/bezahlen/vertreten/
bezeichnen/erklären/verlangen/verkaufen/registrieren/

Erweitern Sie Ihren Wortschatz!

A. Englisch-Deutsch

1. side _____

2. hat _____

3. neighbor _____

4. conductor _____

5. uniform _____

6. bridge _____

7. capital city _____

8. coal _____

9. passport _____

10. economy _____

11. shoe _____

12. to fish _____

13. to make easy _____

14. to be surprised _____

15. to demand _____

16. to vote, elect _____

17. unemployed _____

18. proper, neat _____

19. brown _____

20. independent _____

21. hard-working, industrious _____

22. so-called _____

23. black _____

24. Attention! _____

25. So what? _____

B. Deutsch-Englisch

1. die Fahrkarte _____

2. die Wehrpflicht _____

3. der Bauch _____

4. die Richtung _____

5. das Verhältnis _____

6. die Währung _____

7. das Zeichen _____

8. die Kunst _____

9. die Staatsbürgerschaft _____

10. die Steuer _____

11. der Bundeskanzler _____

12. verhaften _____

13. regieren _____

14. beschreiben _____

15. aufpassen _____

16. aufmachen _____

17. anschließen _____

18. rufen _____

19. sparsam _____

20. eng _____

21. sag' mal _____

22. weiter _____

23. gewisse _____

24. miteinander _____

25. kein Wunder _____

Hör zu . . .und antworte!   Antwortbogen

Übung A. *Circle* **Richtig** *or* **Falsch.**

1. R F	2. R F	3. R F	4. R F	5. R F	6. R F
7. R F	8. R F	9. R F	10. R F	11. R F	12. R F
13. R F	14. R F	15. R F	16. R F	17. R F	18. R F
19. R F	20. R F	21. R F	22. R F		

Übung B. *Circle A, B, or C. More than one answer may be correct.*

1. A B C	2. A B C	3. A B C	4. A B C
5. A B C	6. A B C	7. A B C	8. A B C
9. A B C	10. A B C	11. A B C	12. A B C
13. A B C	14. A B C	15. A B C	16. A B C
17. A B C	18. A B C	19. A B C	20. A B C
21. A B C			

Kapitel 18

Selbst-Test

DIALOG

Translate the underlined expressions.

1. <u>Was werden wir später mit all den</u> vom Öl abhängenden <u>Dingen machen</u>?

   — What will we do later with all those things

2. <u>Über diese viel diskutierten Probleme</u> stellten wir verschiedene Fragen.

   — About these much-discussed problems

3. <u>Die immer größer werdende Menge von Atommüll</u>

   — The amount of atomic waste that is growing bigger and bigger

4. Ich bin <u>mit den in den letzten Jahren gemachten Fortschritten</u> zufrieden.

   — with the progress made in the last years

5. <u>In den schon gebauten Kernkraftwerken</u>

   — In the nuclear power plants already built

6. <u>Das heute viel zitierte Wort „Umweltschutz"</u>

   — The word "environmental protection", much quoted nowadays

7. Ich denke an <u>die immer strenger werdenden Gesetze.</u>

   — the laws that are becoming stricter and stricter

8. Was sind <u>die damit verbundenen Probleme?</u>

   — the problems connected with it

1. Long attributes

9. A long attribute consists of a present or past _____ plus an additional modifying phrase.

— participle

10. The present or past participle functions as a (limiting/descriptive) adjective.

— descriptive

11. The long attribute (follows/precedes) the noun that it modifies.

— precedes

12. A telltale sign for the beginning of a long attribute is a **der**-word or an **ein**-word followed by a _____.

— preposition

13. Step 1 in deciphering a long attribute consists of identifying the _____ that is being modified.

— noun

14. Step 2 consists of identifying the _____ word that goes with the noun.

— introductory

15. Step 3 consists of identifying the words between the introductory word and the noun. These words constitute the _____ _____.

— long attribute

16. In English, the long attribute is often represented as a _____ clause.

— relative

17. Long attributes (may also/cannot) be expressed in German as relative clauses.

— may also

What is the introductory word to the long attribute?

18. Er beschrieb die von Wernher von Braun gebaute V-2. _____

— die

19. Es wohnten viele Menschen in den durch die V-2 terrorisierten Städten Englands. _____

— den

20. ,,Meine für die Mondforschung gebaute Rakete wird jetzt für den Krieg verwendet,'' meinte von Braun später. _____

— Meine

What is the noun that is being modified?

21. Er beschrieb die von Wernher von Braun gebaute V-2. _____

— V-2

22. Es wohnten viele Menschen in den durch die V-2 terrorisierten Städten Englands. _____

— Städten

23. ,,Meine für die Mondforschung gebaute Rakete wird jetzt für den Krieg verwendet,'' meinte von Braun später. _____

— Rakete

24. The noun modified may sometimes be preceded by an additional _____ or _____.

— adjective, adverb

What is the long attribute?

25. Es war im Jahre 1950, als die für die US-Armee von von Braun entwickelte neue Rakete zum ersten Mal startete. _____

— für die US-Armee von von Braun entwickelte

26. In the preceding sentence, the noun modified by the long attribute is preceded by the adjective _____.

— neue

Complete the information on the basis of the Lesestück *for Chapter 18.*

27. Das Deutsche Reich wurde im Jahre 1871 von _____ gegründet.

— Otto von Bismarck

28. Der Zweite Weltkrieg endete im Jahre _____.

— 1945

29. Bald nach dem Ende des Weltkrieges entwickelte sich der _____ Krieg zwischen den Mächten des Ostens und des Westens.

— Kalte

30. Durch die Gründung der BRD und DDR im Jahre 1949 wurde Deutschland ein _____Land.

— geteiltes

31. Die BRD besteht aus _____ Ländern und _____.

— zehn, Westberlin

32. Die BRD hat etwa _____ Millionen Einwohner.

— 63

33. Seit den sechziger Jahren ist das Verhältnis zwischen den Oststaaten und der BRD _____.

— normalisiert

34. In den fünfziger Jahren begann das deutsche Wirtschafts _____.

— wunder

35. Durch den „numerus clausus" ist die Zahl der _____ beschränkt.

— Studienplätze (*or* Studenten)

36. Das Motte „_____, _____, _____" ist heute nicht mehr modern.

— Kinder, Küche, Kirche

37. Der Süden der BRD ist meistens _____; im Norden gibt es mehr _____.

— katholisch, Protestanten

38. Wie andere Staaten hat auch die BRD ihre _____.

— Probleme

39. Die DDR ist etwa so groß wie der amerikanische Staat

— Virginia

40. Sie hat etwa _____ Einwohner.

— 17 Millionen

41. Die Führung des Staates liegt in den Händen des _____ und der _____ _____ _____ (SED).

— Politbüros, Sozialistischen Einheitspartei Deutschlands

42. Im Jahre 1970 nahmen die BRD und die DDR diplomatische _____ auf.

— Beziehungen

43. Heute ist die DDR ein Mitglied der _____ Nationen.

— Vereinten

44. Die Grenze zwischen der BRD und DDR ist _____ Kilometer lang.

— 544

45. Zwischen 1945 und 1961 sind fast _____ Millionen trotz der „Mauer" nach Westdeutschland geflüchtet.

— drei

46. Wirtschaftlich zählt heute die DDR zu den _____ führenden Industrieländern der Welt.

— zehn

47. Der Sport in der DDR wird von der _____ finanziert.
48. Die Landwirtschaft in der DDR ist _____.
49. Fast alle Studenten in der DDR bekommen _____.
50. Pflichtfächer sind die Philosophie des _____ und des _____ sowie _____.
51. Die meisten DDR-Bürger gehören der _____ Kirche an.

52. Die DDR betont die _____ der Frau.
53. Wie in der BRD liegt auch die Zahl der Geburten in der DDR unter dem _____.
54. Der steigende Lebensstandard der DDR ist ein

    _____ _____.
55. Viele DDR-Bürger möchten ihre Verwandten und _____ im Westen besuchen, aber dürfen es nicht.
56. Udo Lindenberg ist ein populärer _____.
57. Der Tagesschein ist bis _____ Uhr gültig (valid).

58. Beide, das Mädchen aus Ostberlin und der Junge aus Westberlin, wollen nur einfach _____.

— Regierung
— kollektiviert
— Stipendien
— Marxismus, Leninismus, Russisch
— protestantischen (or evangelischen)
— Gleichberechtigung

— Nullwachstum

— Erfolg

— Freunde
— Liedermacher
— zwölf, d.h. vierundzwanzig

— zusammensein

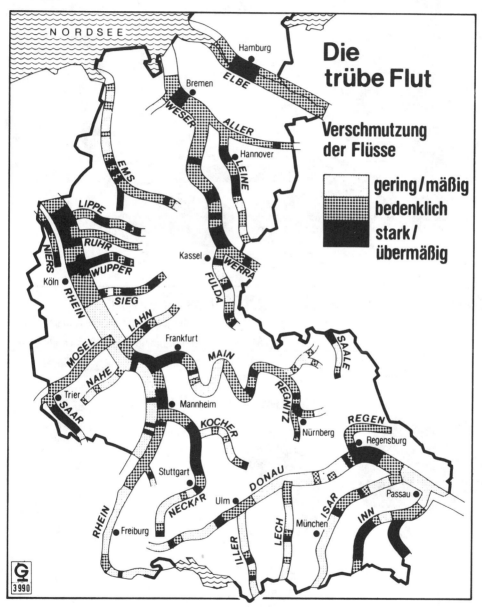

NORDSEE

Hamburg

Bremen

ELBE

WESER

ALLER

Hannover

EMS

LEINE

LIPPE

NIERS

RUHR

WUPPER

Köln

Kassel

WERRA

RHEIN

SIEG

FULDA

MOSEL

LAHN

Frankfurt

MAIN

SAALE

NAHE

Trier

Mannheim

REGNITZ

SAAR

KOCHER

REGEN

Nürnberg

Regensburg

Stuttgart

DONAU

Ulm

ISAR

Passau

RHEIN

NECKAR

Freiburg

ILLER

LECH

München

INN

Die trübe Flut

Verschmutzung der Flüsse

- gering / mäßig
- bedenklich
- stark / übermäßig

G
3 990

Source: Inter Nationes.

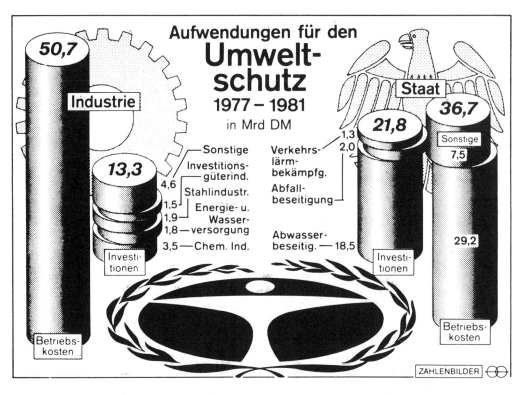

Aufwendungen für den Umwelt-schutz
1977 – 1981
in Mrd DM

Industrie 50,7

Staat 36,7

21,8

13,3

— Sonstige
— Investitions-güterind. 4,6
— Stahlindustr. 1,5
— Energie- u. Wasser-versorgung 1,9
1,8 —
3,5 — Chem. Ind.

Investi-tionen

Betriebs-kosten

Verkehrs-lärm-bekämpfg. 1,3
Abfall-beseitigung 2,0

Abwasser-beseitig. — 18,5

Sonstige 7,5

29,2

Investi-tionen

Betriebs-kosten

ZAHLENBILDER

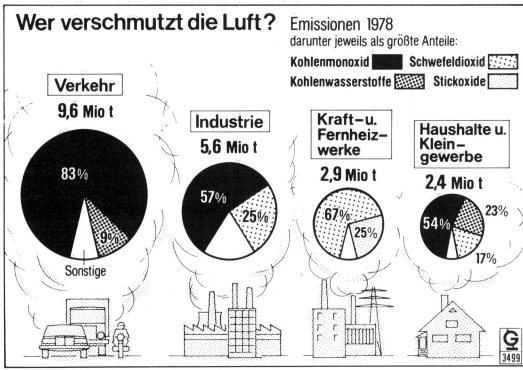

Wer verschmutzt die Luft?

Emissionen 1978
darunter jeweils als größte Anteile:

Kohlenmonoxid █   Schwefeldioxid
Kohlenwasserstoffe   Stickoxide

Verkehr
9,6 Mio t
83%
9%
Sonstige

Industrie
5,6 Mio t
57%
25%

Kraft-u. Fernheiz-werke
2,9 Mio t
67%
25%

Haushalte u. Klein-gewerbe
2,4 Mio t
54%
23%
17%

G 3499

Source: Both, Inter Nationes

Probe-Test

A. *Translate.*

1. Die Alliierten besetzten die von Bomben und Kämpfen zerstörten Städte.

   _____

   _____

2. Im Jahre 1949 wurde aus dem in drei Besatzungszonen aufgeteilten westlichen Teil Deutschlands die BRD.

   _____

   _____

3. Das in den fünfziger Jahren oft zitierte Motto vom ,,Wirtschaftswunder'' hört man heute nicht mehr so oft.

   _____

   _____

4. Wie steht es mit der Stellung der Frau in der Bundesrepublik?

   _____

   _____

5. Das für die westlichen Demokratien nicht zu akzeptierende Prinzip des demokratischen Zentralismus spielt eine große Rolle in der DDR.

_____

_____

_____

6. Die aus etwa zwei Millionen Mitgliedern bestehende SED ist die mächtigste Partei.

_____

_____

7. Die von der Regierung geleitete Planwirtschaft bestimmt alle Aspekte des wirtschaftlichen Lebens.

_____

_____

8. Die außer Haus arbeitende Frau findet die Hilfe des Staates.

_____

_____

B. *Express your opinion in German.*

1. Ich bin (für/gegen) die Kernkraftwerke, weil _____

_____.

2. Es ist (gut/nicht gut), daß die Bundesrepublik ein Mitglied der NATO ist, denn _____

_____

3. Ich (glaube/glaube nicht), daß die DDR „demokratisch" ist, weil _____

_____.

4. Was mir besonders an der (Bundesrepublik Deutschland/Deutschen Demokratischen Republik) gefällt, ist die Tatsache, daß _____

_____

5. Ich hoffe, daß es (wieder/nie wieder) ein einziges Deutschland gibt, weil _____

_____

Erweitern Sie Ihren Wortschatz!

A. Englisch-Deutsch

1. citizen _____

2. thing _____

3. factory _____

4. lake _____

5. environmental protection _____

   _____

6. cost(s) _____

7. border _____

8. kitchen _____

9. goal _____

10. fight, battle _____

11. The German Empire_____

12. division _____

13. to destroy _____

14. to flee, escape _____

15. to protect _____

16. to be hungry, to starve _____

17. to consist _____

18. to work together _____

19. approximately _____

20. economic(ally) _____

21. dependent _____

22. satisfied _____

23. eastern _____

24. to come to an end _____

25. poisonous _____

B. Deutsch-Englisch

1. das Erdgas _____

2. die Ölheizung _____

3. der Atommüll _____

4. die Fußgängerzone _____

5. die Umweltverschmutzung _____

   _____

6. das Schicksal _____

7. der Jude _____

8. die Stellung _____

9. das Wirtschaftswunder _____

10. die Gemeinschaft _____

11. die Verfassung _____

12. die Säuberung _____

13. einführen _____

14. teilen _____

15. trennen _____

16. verschwinden _____

17. gründen _____

18. rechtfertigen _____

19. kinderfreundlich _____

20. sichtbar _____

21. gesamt _____

22. geteilt _____

23. streng _____

24. zuwenig _____

25. zur Kasse bitten . . . ? _____

Hör zu . . . und antworte! Antwortbogen

Übung **A**. *Circle A, B, or C. More than one answer may be correct.*

1. A   B   C   2. A   B   C   3. A   B   C   4. A   B   C

5. A   B   C   6. A   B   C   7. A   B   C   8. A   B   C

9. A   B   C   10. A   B   C

Übung **B**. *Circle A, B, or C.*

1. A   B   C   2. A   B   C   3. A   B   C   4. A   B   C

5. A   B   C   6. A   B   C   7. A   B   C   8. A   B   C

9. A   B   C   10. A   B   C

Übung **C**. *Circle A, B, or C.*

1. A   B   C   2. A   B   C   3. A   B   C   4. A   B   C

5. A   B   C   6. A   B   C   7. A   B   C   8. A   B   C

9. A   B   C   10. A   B   C

Übung **D.** *Circle* **Ja** *or* **Nein.**

1. Ja   Nein   2. Ja   Nein   3. Ja   Nein   4. Ja   Nein   5. Ja   Nein

6. Ja   Nein   7. Ja   Nein   8. Ja   Nein   9. Ja   Nein   10. Ja   Nein

11. Ja   Nein   12. Ja   Nein   13. Ja   Nein   14. Ja   Nein   15. Ja   Nein

Anhang

Review of errors often made by English-speaking students of German

This review covers items introduced in all the chapters of the text and a few new ones. The "errors" to which special attention is drawn in this review are caused by such linguistic phenomena as look-alikes (German **also** means *therefore,* not *also*); sound-alikes (**wer** *who* and *where* **wo**); and interference, that is the transference of English speaking habits to German. Other errors are caused by nuances between German words (**wissen** and **kennen**).

Express in German.

wo, wohin, or **woher**?

1. Where do you live? _____

2. Where are you going? _____

3. Where do you come from? _____

wenn, wann, or **als**?

4. When do you have time? _____

5. If it rains, I'll stay at home. _____

6. I lived in Germany when I was young. _____

7. Did she say when she would come? _____

8. If I have money, I'll buy it. _____

9. When I arrived, he was already here. _____

Zeit, Uhr, or **Stunde?**

10. What time is it? _____

11. Do you have a watch? _____

12. It is still time. _____

13. I'll come in one hour. _____

denn or **dann?**

14. I can't come, for I have no time. _____

15. Now we'll eat and then we'll go home. _____

nach Hause or **zu Hause?**

16. I am living at home. _____

17. Are you going home? _____

das or **daß?**

18. That is not right. _____

19. I say that this is not right. _____

20. That is a good idea! _____

21. I don't believe that. _____

22. He says that he can't come. _____

wollen or **werden?**

23. I want to go home. _____

24. I will go home. _____

25. He wants to buy it. _____

26. Will he buy it? _____

nur or **erst?**

27. There is only one answer. _____

28. I received the answer only yesterday. _____

29. This car is only two years old. _____

30. He has been studying German for only one year. _____

Zahl or **Nummer?**

31. My house number is eleven. _____

32. The number of students is great. _____

33. My number is in the telephone book. _____

34. One is the first number. _____

muß or **mußte?**

35. I must go home. _____

36. I had to go home. _____

37. I had to do it. _____

38. Must you do it? _____

sehen or **aussehen?**

39. You look well. _____

40. Can you see well? _____

41. It looks as if it might rain. _____

nach *toward* and **nach** *according to*

42. I am going home. _____

43. After school, I'll go home. _____

44. That is the custom according to old tradition. _____

da *here* and **da** *since*

45. I am here! _____

46. He is here. _____

47. Since you are here, all is well. _____

vor or **bevor**?

48. A few years ago, I was in Germany. _____

49. Before I came to America, I lived in Germany. _____

50. I am standing before the door. _____

hören or **gehören**?

51. Have you heard the news? _____

52. To whom does this book belong? _____

wissen or **kennen**?

53. I know this man. _____

54. I know the address. _____

55. I know it. _____

56. I know the answer. _____

aber or **sondern?**

57. I live here, but work in Munich. _____

58. He is not dumb, but very intelligent. _____

59. He was hungry, but wanted nothing to eat. _____

60. That was not yesterday, but last Sunday. _____

rufen or **anrufen?**

61. I'll call you (on the phone). _____

62. Who called my name? _____

63. Call the police! _____

Sie or **Ihnen?**

64. What is your name? _____

65. How are you? _____

66. I am fine. And you? _____

heißen or **nennen?**

67. I am called Fritz. _____

68. Name me two famous scientists. _____

69. What's Munich called in German? _____

70. We have a new dog. What shall we call him? _____

selbst *self* and **selbst** *even*

71. He came in person. _____

72. Even he came. _____

73. He can do it himself. _____

74. Even he knows the answer. _____

vorstellen or **sich vorstellen**?

75. I can imagine that. _____

76. He introduced himself. _____

77. May I introduce myself? _____

78. I can't imagine what that means. _____

hier or **hierher**?

79. Do you live here? _____

80. Come here! _____

81. Here is your book. _____

82. Put it here! _____

dort or **dorthin**?

83. He lives there. _____

84. I am going there. _____

85. There is our house. _____

86. You have to write there. _____

hin or **her**?

87. Come here! _____

88. Go there! _____

89. Walk back and forth! _____

schwer *difficult* and **schwer** *heavy*

90. This work is difficult. _____

91. This suitcase is heavy. _____

leben or **wohnen**?

92. They live in this house. _____

93. They live in Germany. _____

94. Where do you live? _____

95. They live well. _____

mutig or **brav**?

96. He is courageous. _____

97. This is a good child. _____

98. She is brave. _____

99. Be good! _____

meinen or **bedeuten**?

100. What does it mean? _____

101. I mean it differently. _____

102. What do you mean? _____

103. This means nothing. _____

zählen, erzählen, or **zahlen**?

104. He is counting his money. _____

105. He is telling a joke. _____

106. We are paying the bill. _____

fahren *to travel* and **fahren** *to drive, to ride*

107. We are taking the train. _____

108. We are traveling to Germany. _____

109. He drives to school. _____

110. When does the bus depart? _____

bekommen or **werden**?

111. The rich are becoming richer. _____

112. What am I getting for Christmas? _____

113. She is (in the process of) becoming a doctor. _____

114. When do we receive a visit? _____

115. When do we receive our money? _____

heiß or **scharf**?

116. The knife is sharp. _____

117. The weather is hot. _____

118. Mexican food is hot. _____

119. Hot coffee is good. _____

Translate into English. Watch for the underlined items!

120. Wir kommen <u>also</u> um fünf Uhr. _____

121. Seine <u>Art</u> zu sprechen, gefällt mir nicht. _____

122. Dieses <u>Gift</u> ist sehr gefährlich. _____

123. Es regnet, <u>also</u> bleiben wir zu Haus. _____

124. Ingrid <u>bekam</u> keine Antwort. _____

125. Ich habe das oft <u>gehört</u>. _____

126. Hans <u>bittet</u> mich um Geld. _____

127. Er <u>fragt</u> nach der Zeit. _____

128. Ich bin so groß <u>wie</u> er. _____

129. Er ist größer <u>als</u> Ulrike. _____

130. <u>Als</u> wir in Deutschland lebten, war es nicht so teuer. _____

131. Er tut, <u>als ob</u> er reich wäre. _____

132. Das <u>gehört</u> mir nicht. _____

133. Ich habe keinen Job; <u>also</u> habe ich auch kein Geld. _____

134. Er ist sicher hier, <u>da</u> ich ihn heute schon gesehen habe. _____

135. <u>Da</u> ist er ja! _____

136. Darüber kann ich weder <u>lachen</u> noch <u>lächeln</u>. _____

_____

137. Das macht <u>nichts</u>. _____

138. Es tut mir leid, aber ich habe <u>nichts</u> gesehen. _____

139. Ich kann <u>mich</u> gut an ihn <u>erinnern</u>. _____

140. Er <u>erinnert mich</u> an meinen Freund Karl. _____

141. Wie schön, daß heute wieder die Sonne <u>scheint</u>. _____

142. Es <u>scheint</u> uns, als hätten sie wieder alles vergessen. _____

143. Morgen <u>holen</u> wir <u>wieder</u> Geld von der Bank. _____

144. Die Klasse <u>wiederholt</u> heute den Konjunktiv. _____

English equivalents of the Dialogs

CHAPTER 1

What's her name? And who is she?

Günter Müller Hans, do you know the girl there?
Hans Mayer No, I don't know her. Who is she?
G. Her name is Ursula Schwartz; she is a student.
H. What is she studying?
G. She is studying medicine. And she is very nice! (*Miss Schwarz comes.*)
G. Hello, Ursula, how are you?
Ursula Schwarz Fine, thanks. And you?
G. Thanks. I am fine, too. —Ursula, this is Hans Mayer.
U. Hello, Mr. Mayer. Are you a student, too?
H. Yes, I am studying biology.
G. . . . and he likes to dance, he has a lot of records, is learning karate, plays tennis, and . . .
U. Tennis? I like to play tennis, too, but unfortunately I don't play very well.
G. Ursula, are you coming to the concert tonight?
U. I don't think so. I haven't time today. And [I've got] a lot of work! (*The bus comes.*) —Here is the bus. Good-bye!
H. and G. Good-bye.

CHAPTER 2

Thanks a lot for the information

Mr. Kaufmann Mr. Wertheim, how do I get from here to Beethoven-Street?
Mr. Wertheim Are you on foot or do you have a car?
Mr. K. I am on foot today. I like to walk.
Mr. W. It's quite far on foot. Why don't you take the streetcar? The "seven" goes that way.

Mrs. Wertheim	Hold it, Hans, the "seven" only goes as far as Bismarck Avenue. But from there there's now a bus.
Mr. W.	Do you know that for sure?
Mrs. W.	Yes, I go there often. The bus leaves every fifteen minutes.
Mr. W.	I believe you are right. (*looks at the street*) What? It's raining again. What weather! And you don't have an umbrella!
Mr. K.	That doesn't matter. I have a raincoat.
Mrs. W.	I just hope you won't get all wet. You know this is the flu season.
Mr. K.	Don't worry, rain doesn't bother me. Thanks a lot for the information.
Mr. W.	Don't mention it. Good-bye!
Mr. K.	Good-bye!

CHAPTER 3

A small crisis
(or: If one doesn't read the timetable correctly)

Characters	Fritz Richter
	a passer-by
	a young woman at the information booth
Place	The railroad station at Nuremberg

Mr. Richter is in a hurry. He sees that there is a train standing on Track One. He asks a passer-by.

Mr. Richter	Excuse me, is this the train to Cologne?
Passer-by	The train to Cologne? That I don't know. Do you see the sign "Information" there? Ask there.
Mr. R.	Where? (*looks to the left*) I don't see any sign.
P.	No, not there. Over there. Look to the right, not to the left.
Mr. R.	Oh yes, now I see it. Thanks a lot. (*quickly runs on and finds the information booth*) Hello! Excuse me, where is the express train to Cologne? It leaves at 8 P.M.
Young woman	Express train to Cologne? There's no express train going to Cologne today.
Mr. R.	That's not possible! Here is the timetable. Read what it says there, please: Express train to Cologne. Departure from Nuremberg at 8 P.M.
Young woman	(*reads the timetable*) I am sorry. But the train only runs on weekdays. Today is Sunday.
Mr. R.	Oh, my God. What am I going to do now?
Young woman	Fly, if you're in such a hurry.
Mr. R.	How much does it cost?
Young woman	120 Marks.
Mr. R.	Is there still a flight to Cologne today?
Young woman	(*looks at the clock*) Yes, in 40 minutes.

Mr. R.	Do you think I'll still get a seat?
Young woman	Perhaps. Just a moment please. I'll call Lufthansa. (*She calls.*) Yes. Lufthansa flight 219 still has seats.
Mr. R.	Do I still have enough time? The airport is pretty far from here, isn't it?
Young woman	No problem, if you take a taxi.
Mr. R.	Thanks a lot!
Young woman	Have a good flight!

CHAPTER 4

How large, how far, how much . . .?

A. How well do you know the metric system?

B. Pretty well, I think.

A. Okay, for example: What do you think? How large in diameter is an aspirin tablet, in millimeters of course?

B. Oh, I don't know that.

A. Guess

B. I believe perhaps [. . .] millimeters.

A. Excuse me, please. How tall do you think Miss [. . .], Mr. [. . .], Mrs. [. . .] is? Naturally in meters and centimeters.

B. Stand up, please. — Hm, I think you're . . . tall.

A. Let's measure her (him). Not bad; she's [. . .], he's [. . .] tall.

A. Do you like to swim?

B. Oh yes, if the water isn't too cold—and the air either.

A. Is it too cold for you if the temperature of the water is twenty degrees Celsius? And if the temperature of the air is 25 degrees Celsius? How cold or warm is that in Fahrenheit?

B. (uses a pocket calculator) Just a second. I know [. . .] Twenty degrees Celsius are [. . .] degrees Fahrenheit, and 25 degrees Celsius are [. . .] degrees Fahrenheit.

A. Too cold?

B. No, that's all right.

A. Do you see the Volkswagen over there?

B. Yes, I see it.

A. A VW needs a gallon for thirty miles. How much is that in liters and kilometers?

B. Just a minute. How do I figure that out?

A. A gallon holds about 3.7 liters.

B. And one mile is about 1.6 kilometers.

A. Right!

B. So, that means: The VW needs 3.7 liters per 30 times 1.6 kilometers. That comes to 48 kilometers. So, 7.4 liters for not quite 100 kilometers—or 96 kilometers, exactly.

CHAPTER 5

Are marriage ads [to be taken] seriously?

Petra Fischer, a young German student, and John Taylor, a young American, are sitting at a table in a pastry shop.

John (He shows her a newspaper and shakes his head.) This is incredible! Are these people kidding, Petra?

Petra What are you talking about? And about whom?

J. About the marriage ads in the newspaper. We don't have anything like that in America.

P. You mean you don't have any marriage ads at all? Not in any paper?

J. Oh well, they do exist. But marriage ads in a newspaper don't seem very proper to us.

P. Not proper? Doesn't that depend upon the newspaper and the ad? Here you find marriage ads in the "Welt," in the "Tagesspiegel," and in the "Salzburger Nachrichten." Those are very decent newspapers, aren't they?

J. Certainly, but I don't understand why people are looking for a partner in the paper.

P. Why not?

J. What's the matter with them? Do they have complexes?

P. You do these people wrong.

J. No, no, I don't mean it that way. But marriage ads in the newspapers. . . . They don't belong there!

P. Other countries, other customs!

J. I also don't think it's very nice when women place ads this way.

P. Aha, typical! Male chauvinism: The girl waits patiently for the prince.

J. I'm sorry if you understand it that way. But do you really believe that marriage ads help women?

P. Not only women. Men, too! Whoever is alone, looks for contact.

J. Yes, I know . . .

CHAPTER 6

Difficult decisions

Gisela and Karin are sitting at a table in the dormitory.

Gisela So you want to live together next semester, you and Walter.

Karin Perhaps. It's Walter's idea. He wants me to live with him.

G. And what about you? Don't you want to?

K. I don't know . . . Perhaps we should wait a bit.

G. Living together surely has advantages for you too: then you can study together, you can be together more often, you . . .

K. Well, yes, that's right. And we can also save money. But think of the problem with our parents. I don't know if they can accept that.

G. Why not? You do want to get married later.

K. Just a minute. Living together doesn't mean that you have to get married.

G. But Walter would like to marry you.

K. Of course, but I don't know if I want to yet. I'd like to stay independent still.

G. (*Looks at her watch.*) Well, Karin, I have to go now. See you later!

Herbert and Walter are sitting in Walter's two-room apartment.

Herbert Walter, is it true that Karin is going to live with you next semester? Great!

Walter Yes, perhaps. She wants to live with me.

H. And what do Karin's parents say? Is she allowed to do that?

W. What do I know? We want to save money.

H. Sure, if you need only one apartment and one car, then you can save money. You want to get married soon, don't you?

W. Get married? That can wait. That's Karin's idea.

H. Hold it, she's such a nice girl, isn't she?

W. That's right. But I'd like to stay independent still.

CHAPTER 7

We are in no hurry

Characters Mrs. Elisabeth Keller (Liselotte's mother)
Mrs. Liselotte Stein (Mrs. Keller's married daughter)

Mother Liselotte, how long have you been married now?

Daughter It's going to be three years this fall.

M. What, that long? How time flies!
Have you read this article? (*points to the newspaper*)

D. Which one?

M. Here, about "zero population growth."

D. Zero population growth?

M. Yes, last year the population in Germany decreased again.

D. Aha, now I understand! So you were probably thinking about Klaus and me.

M. Not directly, but I already had two children after three years (of marriage).

D. But that doesn't mean that every couple has to have kids after three years.

M. I didn't say that, but you do want a family. Or don't you?

D. Believe me, Mom, Klaus and I have already talked about this topic often.

M. And . . . ?

D. We're not in such a hurry. Until now we've had other plans. I earned some additional money, we saved for a new car, we traveled a lot, and . . .

M. . . . and I haven't got any grandchildren yet!

D. (*with her arm around her mother*) Mother, you know the saying: "What hasn't happened yet can still happen . . ."

CHAPTER 8

Do you know these famous people? A little quiz

A. This Austrian woman wrote a famous book in 1889. The title was *Lay Down Your Arms.*

B. Was this book a protest against war?

A. Right. And I'll give you another clue. The author also knew Alfred Nobel, the inventor of dynamite.

C. Nobel? Didn't he later donate the money for the Nobel Prize?

A. You're right. This woman gave Alfred Nobel the idea for the Nobel Peace Prize.

D. Didn't she receive the Nobel Peace Prize? I believe, that was in 1905.

A. Right!

D. Now I know her name. This woman was . . .

A. This German was professor of physics at Würzburg University. He discovered unknown rays there.

B. When did he teach there?

A. From 1888 until 1899. He made his discovery in November 1895.

C. Was it an important discovery?

A. Yes, especially for medicine.

D. Aha! Did he want to find these rays or was his discovery a coincidence?

A. I believe it was a coincidence. And he was lucky.

E. Were the rays later given the name of the professor?

A. Yes, that's correct. The professor became famous.

G. Well, then everything's clear. We're speaking about Professor . . .

CHAPTER 9

Tennis or "stay fit"

Characters Uwe Baumann, a student from Germany. (He has been in America for two weeks.)
Craig Norton, an American student.

Place In the dormitory

Uwe Good morning, Craig! Sleep well?

Craig Thanks, pretty well.

Uwe And how are you today? I heard you were sick.

Craig Yes, I had a cold. But I'm already playing tennis again.

Uwe Tennis? How long have you been playing?

Craig Oh, for half a year. It's fun! Do you play too?

Uwe No, I don't have enough money for that. I can't afford tennis. It's an expensive sport, isn't it?

Craig I believe you're mistaken there. Perhaps that's true in Germany, but not here in America. You only need a racket, a few tennis balls, and then you can play.

Uwe Don't you have to belong to a club? And that costs quite a bit, doesn't it?

Craig Oh no, on the public courts and at the university it doesn't cost anything, or not much.

Uwe But don't you have to wait a long time until a court is free? I'd rather jog.

Craig You run? Are you a jogger?

Uwe Yes, I started with that a few years ago in Germany. There they now have outdoor physical fitness trails everywhere.

Craig Yes, I've heard about that. You run through a forest or a park. And don't you also do some calisthenics along with it?

Uwe Yes, you do, a few knee-bends and push-ups, and so on.

Craig Do you run every day?

Uwe No, but three times a week. And early in the morning, before I shower and shave.

Craig And how far (do you run)?

Uwe Oh, about three to four kilometers.

Craig But that's boring! I think I'll stick to my tennis.

Uwe And I to my jogging!

CHAPTER 10

What will the twenty-first century bring?

A German newspaper put this question to students and professors on the campus of Bremen University. Here are their answers:

Reporter What do you think; what will the twenty-first century bring us?

Christa Lenz We will have a lot more leisure time than now.

Reporter And what will one do with the leisure time?

Christa Lenz I believe people will have more time for their families and their hobbies. People will travel more, but also watch more television—and, I hope, read more.

Reporter What is your prognosis for the next century?

Heinz-Loeb I believe above all that they will explore new planets in the twenty-first century. And robots will do the work in the factories.

Reporter And what do you think about that?

Heinz-Loeb That's good! I really believe that people will have a better life. The quality of life will get better.

Reporter And what is your opinion about the future in the next century?

Professor Schumann If there is going to be a twenty-first century, we will have to be lucky.

Reporter How am I supposed to understand that?

Professor Schumann I'm not sure whether we will live to see the twenty-first century.

Reporter And why not?

Professor Schumann Haven't you ever heard of the arms race and nuclear war?

Reporter Oh, that's it. I didn't think you would be so pessimistic about the future.

CHAPTER 11

You, you are in my heart . . .

*The German writer Gerhart Hauptmann (1862-1946) became famous in 1889
with his first drama "Before Sunrise." The "Free Stage" theater in Berlin was
the first theater in Germany to perform this controversial avant-garde play.
"Before Sunrise" led to loud protests and even to a big theater scandal. This
play paved the way for Naturalism in Germany. Gerhart Hauptmann received
the Nobel Prize for Literature in 1912.*

*Here we present a short excerpt—with some small changes—from "Before
Sunrise." Alfred Loth meets young Helene Krause. It is a love scene; the
scene shows the important step from "Sie" to "du" in the German language.
This step played an important role then—just as it still does today.*

Helene	(leading him to a quiet arbor) In the arbor, I think . . . It's my favorite spot. Here we won't be disturbed.
Loth	A pretty place here—really! (Both sit down. Silence.) You have such beautiful, rich hair, Miss!
Helene	If I loosen it, it reaches down to my knees. Feel it!
Loth	Just like silk. (kisses her hair)
Helene	Please, don't! If . . .
Loth	Helene—! Weren't you serious before?
Helene	Oh! I'm so terribly ashamed of myself . . . What have I done? I've forced myself upon you. What must you think of me?
Loth	Please don't say such a thing! (She kisses him on the mouth first. Both blush, then Loth returns the kiss.) Lene, right? They call you Lene here, don't they?
Helene	(kisses him) Call me something else . . . Call me whatever you'd really like.
Loth	Darling!
Helene	(her head resting on his chest) Oh! How wonderful! How wonderful!

CHAPTER 12

The power of advertising

Petra	Inge, may I use your toothpaste? I didn't bring mine along.
Inge	But of course. As it says in the ad: You'll get the whitest teeth from mine.
Petra	Oh sure, and each brand is supposedly the best, the healthiest, the . . .
Inge	And we're dumb enough to believe it all.
Petra	Believe? . . . No, we don't even need to do that. Just as long as we buy, buy, buy.
Inge	You know, I'm really fed up with all the commercials. And every year they get more aggressive and worse.
Petra	. . . and more vulgar.
Inge	Yes, but unfortunately it can't be changed. The fact is: the more advertising, the more buyers.

Petra	I agree, advertising manipulates us.
Inge	That's not quite true. We allow ourselves to be manipulated by commercials.

CHAPTER 13

Will Eberhard get the job?

Characters	Eberhard Schuster, graduate of a Gymnasium
	Mrs. Elisabeth Hartwig, head of personnel
	Mrs. Lange, a secretary
Place	In the office of a large department store

E. Schuster	Hello! My name is Schuster. I would like to speak to Mrs. Hartwig.
Mrs. Lange	Excuse me, what was the name?
E. Schuster	Schuster, Eberhard Schuster.
Mrs. Lange	Ah, you're the young man who is applying for the position in customer service.
E. Schuster	Yes, that's me.
Mrs. Lange	Just a moment, please. I'll tell Mrs. Hartwig that you're here. (*telephones*) Straight ahead, first door to the left.
Mrs. Hartwig	Hello, I am Mrs. Hartwig. Please have a seat. (*looks at his application and his résumé*) I see you graduated from high school in July.
E. Schuster	Yes, from the Pestalozzi-Gymnasium.
Mrs. Hartwig	And even with very good grades. Congratulations! So, you want to work in customer service with us. What interests you particularly there?
E. Schuster	Well, I would like to have lots of contact with people. That's what I'd like. I wouldn't want a job in which one only sits behind a desk.
Mrs. Hartwig	But that's part of customer service, also. Can you type?
E. Schuster	Not very well. There was no course for it in the school which I attended.
Mrs. Hartwig	Well, that doesn't matter. You can still learn it. There are evening classes for that. Incidentally, did you get our information sheet?
E. Schuster	You mean the one with everything about salary, working hours, vacation, and insurance?
Mrs. Hartwig	Yes, that's the one I mean.
E. Schuster	Yes, I read it.
Mrs. Hartwig	Do you have any further questions?
E. Schuster	I don't believe so.—Oh, yes; by when will I find out if I get the job?
Mrs. Hartwig	Probably by Friday. Call me here at the office between 2 and 4 P.M. By the way, you have very good letters of recommendation.
E. Schuster	Thank you very much. Good-bye! (*gets up and wants to go*)
Mrs. Hartwig	Mr. Schuster, isn't that your umbrella?
E. Schuster	Yes, that's mine. That's something I don't generally leave behind. Thanks a lot.
Mrs. Hartwig	Good-bye, Mr. Schuster.

CHAPTER 14

Was it worth it?
(The first moon landing)

Characters   Emil Lange, the host of a talk show at Radio Bremen.
A, B, C, D, E: five callers

Lange   Dear listeners, today is the anniversary of a historic event. On this day in 1969 the American astronauts Neil Armstrong and "Buzz" Aldrin had landed on the moon. Was it worth it? Today we want to discuss this topic. Call us if you want to say something about it. Our telephone number is 75-72-66. Area code 421.

(first call)

A.   I am of the opinion that the moon landing was a big step forward for science. What all didn't they invent for it! Just great!

Lange   Apropos "big step forward": Do you still remember what Armstrong (had) said when he took the first step on the moon?

A.   Yes, something like "one small step for man, but a giant leap for mankind."

Lange   That's right! And millions heard it at the time. Thanks a lot. Here's another call.

(second call)

B.   I was one of those who were sitting in front of the television set at that time. At 3 a.m.! No doubt the moon landing was a remarkable achievement, and I too (had) admired the courage of the astronauts. But I still believe that the Americans had false priorities.

Lange   What do you mean by that?

B.   Well, for instance, I'm thinking of the slums in the large cities, in New York or in Detroit. I had seen them myself on my trip through America! Terrible! For the slums one could never find enough money, but for the moon landing they spent billions. Aren't these false priorities?

(third call)

C.   I believe that the moon landing was no luxury. We all benefit from it.

Lange   Can you explain that please?

C.   Gladly. Just one example: The satellites which they (had) developed for this project today help in weather reports, and the meteorologists too. And let's not forget that this project also aided the development of computer technology.

Lange   Yes, you are right. They (had) developed many new computers for it. But the question of priorities is still a good question. —Here is another call.

(fourth call)

D.   I am in agreement with the lady who spoke about false priorities. There are so many more important things to do than fly to the moon.

Lange   For instance?

D. In many countries people are dying of hunger, there is a population explosion, air pollution, and now also the energy and water crisis. These problems are important—not only space travel.

Lange Thanks a lot for your comments. Today is the anniversary of the moon landing. We are talking about the topic: Was it worth it? We would like to hear your opinion. Our telephone number is 75-72-66. Area code 421.

(fifth call)

E. I find this discussion quite interesting, but I don't understand why one must always be for or against space travel. Does everything always have to be "either . . . or?" Can't we have space travel, and at the same time solve the problems of our earth . . . ?

CHAPTER 15

Wish list for old and young

As children we wish:
 If I only were already bigger!
 If only we had a dog!
 If only we didn't have to go to bed so early!
 If only I could watch television longer!

As students we say: How nice it would be . . .
 if the course of study weren't so difficult!
 if we didn't have so many tests!
 if only I got a job soon!
 if only I could buy myself a car!

When we are in love, we sometimes think:
 I would be so happy, if she (he) would call me today.
 I know that she (he) would never leave me.
 I would go to the ends of the earth with her (him).
 If only we could get married soon!

As young married people hope,
 that the children were never sick.
 that the rent weren't so high.
 that one could buy more.
 that the parents would visit us more often.

At the age of 40 to 50 one says perhaps:
 If only I had married earlier!
 If only I had never married!
 If only we had more leisure time!
 If only we had traveled more when we were younger.

After fifty one thinks perhaps:

If only we had had more time for the children!
If only I hadn't smoked so much, then I would be healthier now!
If only we had visited our parents more often!
If only I were already retired!

And what does one say, if one is retired?

I wish

we lived in Arizona.

we were still younger.

there were no inflation.

we could travel more.

CHAPTER 16

In court: Who is right?

Characters	A judge, Dr. Franz Reimer
	A policeman, Sergeant Lorenz
	Defendants: Mr. Rüdinger, a motorist
	Miss Lechner, a motorist
Place	The traffic court in Vienna

Judge Case 253: Car accident at the intersection of Josef Street and Lange Gasse on July 25 of this year. Sergeant Lorenz, did you see this accident yourself?

Sergeant No, but I wrote the report on it.

Judge What do you say in your report?

Sergeant Mr. Rüdinger alleged that Miss Lechner didn't pay attention to the red light at Josef Street. She supposedly didn't stop.

Judge And what did Miss Lechner have to say about that?

Sergeant She explained that she had stopped, she hadn't seen the other car, and then she had slowly driven across the intersection when the light turned green. There she was hit by Mr. Rüdinger's car.

Judge Miss Lechner, is the assertion correct that you had not paid attention to the red light?

Miss Lechner No, your Honor, of course I stopped. But you should have seen how fast he drove through the intersection! (*pointing to Mr. Rüdinger*) As if he were on a racetrack!

Mr. Rüdinger Your Honor, that's sheer nonsense! This young lady only acts as if she were innocent. (*pointing to Miss Lechner*) People like *you* shouldn't have a driver's license!

Judge Mr. Rüdinger, how fast were you going?

Mr. Rüdinger Oh, at most thirty-five or forty.

Judge	Sergeant Lorenz, were there witnesses for this accident?
Sergeant	Yes, a Mr. Stein and a Mrs. Götz.
Judge	And what have they stated?
Sergeant	Mr. Stein claims that Miss Lechner didn't stop long enough.
Judge	And Mrs. Götz?
Sergeant	She said that the other car was going very fast.

The judge's verdict

Mr. Rüdinger is found guilty: he could have prevented the accident had he not driven so fast. But the judge also warned Miss Lechner not to start too soon in the future when the light changes from red to green.

CHAPTER 17

(Caption under the cartoon, p. 396: "Faster, Tünnes, if we run next to the First Class, we save even more money.")

The "Tünnes and Schäl" jokes, which are characteristic of Cologne humor, are also a type of joke.

They laugh about themselves

The humor of a country tells us something about the customs of its people, about their relationship to other people and to the world. In a joke tensions are gotten rid of. In a joke one can often say what is otherwise not expressed aloud.

There are different kinds of jokes. For instance, jokes which are associated with certain persons. The Count Bobby jokes from Vienna belong to this category. Count Bobby is the senile Austrian aristocrat type.

Count Bobby is sitting in a train. The conductor comes and wants to see his ticket. "You have a ticket for a trip to Vienna. But we are going to Salzburg," says the conductor. "Does the engineer already know that we are going in the wrong direction?" answers Bobby.

Bobby's friend Freddy sees that Bobby is wearing one black shoe and one brown shoe. Freddy: "But Bobby, how *do* you look?! You've got on one brown shoe and one black shoe?" Bobby "Yes, I was wondering about that, too, earlier. And just imagine, at home I have another pair just like them."

People also like regional jokes: jokes about the fresh Berliner, the somewhat crude Bavarian, and slow East Frisian, etc.

Little Fritz, a boy from Berlin, isn't paying attention at school. He is asked by the teacher if he isn't feeling well. "No," said Fritz, "I am not feeling well at all."

Teacher "Where don't you feel well? In the stomach? In the head?"
Fritz "No, here at school."

Franz the Bavarian doesn't like the Prussians. He is sitting next to one at the Hofbräuhaus. "Hey, you, neighbor," says the Prussian. You're sitting on my hat." "So, what?" replies Franz. "You want to leave already?"

In the East Frisian jokes one finds self-irony, a sign of maturity.

What's the meaning of the stripes on the uniform of East Frisian police officers? One stripe: He can read. Two stripes: He can read and write. Three stripes: He knows someone who can read and write.

Political jokes have always been popular. Here one can make fun of politics and politicians. During the Nazi period, the following joke was told secretly in Germany (a so-called "whisper joke"):

Hey, Fritz was arrested yesterday!" "What, Fritz? Such a good guy. And how come?" "Well, *that's* how come."

And here is something about politics in our time:

A famous soccer player of the Federal Republic of Germany is being interviewed. "Do you know that you are earning more than the Federal Chancellor?" "So, what?" replies the soccer player. "I also play a lot better than he does!"

A West German and an East German are fishing in the Elbe river. The West German is catching many fish, the East German is catching none. The East German yells across the river: "Tell me, why are you catching so many and I'm not catching any?" "It's simple," the West German answers, "the fish on my side are not afraid to open their mouths."

CHAPTER 18

What do you think about it?
The energy crisis
Nuclear power plants
Environmental protection

We asked some Germans and Austrians several questions about these three much-discussed current topics. Here are some of the "pro" and "con" opinions which we heard.

Question What do you think of the energy crisis which allegedly is threatening us? Is it real?

Opinion Of course it exists. Crude oil is coming to an end. What will we do later on with all the things which depend upon oil: with our cars, factories, oil heating systems . . .?

Opinion Until now there still has been no serious energy crisis. We still have lots of coal and enough natural gas in Germany. The most important thing is that we save energy. Science and technology will help us. Besides, new nuclear power plants are still being built.

Question That brings us to another problem which today excites all segments of society, the old as well as the young. Are you for or against nuclear power plants? As we have heard, in Austria they voted against the opening of a nuclear power plant which had already been constructed.

Opinion I am against them. They were built before the problems connected with them had been solved.

Question Which problems do you mean?

Opinion For instance, the ever-increasing amount of atomic waste, which nobody knows where to put. And something else. How do we protect these nuclear power plants against sabotage?

Question What are you thinking about when you talk of sabotage?

Opinion About political terrorists, but also extortionists. What would happen if such people were to get their hands on a nuclear power plant?

Opinion I am for the construction of nuclear power plants because we need them. Certainly, the most essential thing is safety. But everything is being done for that in all the nuclear power plants which have been built so far.

Question What do you think of when you hear the currently so popular word "environmental protection?"

Opinion Oh, of the ever increasing number of pedestrian zones in the cities, of the environmental protection laws against fumes which are becoming stricter and stricter, of the cleaning up of our rivers and lakes.

Question Are you of the opinion that too much or too little is being done for environmental protection?

Opinion One can hardly do too much for environmental protection. But I am satisfied with the progress which has been made during the last few years.

Opinion This is the way I see the problem of environmental pollution: Almost everybody says: Of course, we must do something against smoking chimneys and poisonous exhaust fumes. But only a few are ready to pay the high costs which are connected with it.

Question And who should pay for environmental protection? Industry, the state, the individual citizen?

Opinion All of us! Everyone should pay for the environmental pollution. But unfortunately things are such that in practice everybody would like to give the bill to someone else.

Aussprache Übungen

Each chapter of the textbook contains *Aussprache Übungen* which are recorded on the tape for that chapter along with the Dialog, Exercises, and *Lesestück*.

The following pronunciation program is recorded on a separate reel of tape. It includes the *Aussprache Übungen* from the textbook, plus additional exercises. Using the separate reel of tape and this special script, students may work to improve their pronunciation at varying rates, in accordance with their individual needs or the special directions of their instructor.

The pronunciation program is divided into two parts of 32 segments. The first part (segments 1–18) consists of **consonant sounds**, the second part (segments 19–32) of **vowel sounds**.

CONSONANT SOUNDS

1   German **ach**-sound [x] versus German **ich**-sound [ç]

"Back" after **a, o, u, au**		"Front" after **i, e, eu, l, r**	
acht	*eight*	**mich**	*me*
machen	*to make*	**richtig**	*correct*
Nacht	*night*	**Licht**	*light*
Loch	*hole*	**recht**	*right*
hoch	*high*	**sprechen**	*to speak*
Tochter	*daughter*	**sechzehn**	*sixteen*
Buch	*book*	**euch**	*you, to you*
suchen	*to search*	**echt**	*genuine*
Kuchen	*cake*	**leuchten**	*to light*
auch	*also*	**Milch**	*milk*
rauchen	*to smoke*	**durch**	*through*
brauchen	*to need*	**solch**	*such*

2 German ach-sound [x] versus German ich-sound [ç]

"Back" after **a, o, u, au**

Nacht	*night*
lachen	*to laugh*
schwach	*weak*
Tochter	*daughter*
Koch	*cook*
hoch	*high*
Buch	*book*
Frucht	*fruit*
Zucht	*rearing*
Brauch	*custom*
Rauch	*smoke*
Strauch	*bush*

"Front" after **ä, ö, ü, äu**

Nächte	*nights*
lächeln	*to smile*
schwächer	*weaker*
Töchter	*daughters*
Köchin	*cook* (female)
höchst	*highest*
Bücher	*books*
Früchte	*fruits*
züchten	*to breed, raise*
Bräuche	*customs*
räuchern	*to smoke* (meat)
Sträuche	*bushes*

3 German k, ck [k] versus German ch [x]

nackt	*nude*
(er) **nickt**	*he nods*
Streik	*strike*
(er) **schluckt**	*he swallows*
Säcke	*sacks*
Laken	*sheets*
Dock	*dock*
Locken	*curls*
Rock	*skirt*
Pocken	*smallpox*
(er) **buk**	*he baked*
Bäcker	*baker*
dick	*thick, fat*
(es) **zuckt**	*it twitches*
pauken	*to drum*

Nacht	*night*
nicht	*not*
Streich	*prank*
Schlucht	*canyon*
Sache	*matter*
lachen	*to laugh*
doch	*yet*
lochen	*to punch holes*
(es) **roch**	*it smelled*
pochen	*to knock*
Buch	*book*
Becher	*goblet*
dich	*you*
Zucht	*rearing*
brauchen	*to need*

4 German sch [ʃ] versus German ch [x]

wasch (dich)	*wash yourself*
Kirsche	*cherry*
Mensch	*human being*
Menschen	*people*
wünschen	*to wish*
rauschen	*to roar*

wach (auf)	*wake up*
Kirche	*church*
Mönch	*monk*
Männchen	*little man*
München	*Munich*
rauchen	*to smoke*

waschen	to wash		wachen	to watch, guard
Tisch	table		dich	you
Büsche	bushes		Bücher	books
Rausch	inebriation		Rauch	smoke
Masche	stitch		Mache	sham
Busch	bush		Buch	book
Aschen	ashes		Aachen	German city (Aix-la-Chapelle)

5 German z, tz [ts] versus English z [š]

Whether it occurs at the beginning of a syllable or word or at the end, the sound is the same.

Zahn	tooth	zany	
Schwanz	tail	zombie	
zehn	ten	zenith	
bezahlen	to pay	Zanzibar	
zittern	to tremble	zither	
Zink	zinc	zinc	
Zoo	zoo	zoo	
Zone	zone	zone	
Zug	train	zucchini	
zu	to, closed	Zulu	
beziehen	to subscribe	enzyme	
Zebra	zebra	zebra	
Zickzack	zigzag	zigzag	
zerreißen	to tear	zero	

6 German s [š] or [s] versus German z, tz [ts]

Saal	hall		Zahl	number
sehen	to see		Zehen	toes
seit	since		Zeit	time
Sinn	sense		Zinn	tin
so	so		Zoo	zoo
(er) soll	he should		Zoll	customs
sauber	clean		Zauber	magic
weisen	to direct		Weizen	wheat
heißen	to be called		heizen	to heat
Hessen	Hessia		hetzen	to harass
Kasse	cashier		Katze	cat
Schweiß	sweat		Schweiz	Switzerland
Gans	goose		ganz	whole

Reis	*rice*	**Reiz**	*charm*
reisen	*to travel*	**reizen**	*to incite*

7 German **st** [ʃt] as the initial sound of a word or syllable versus German **st** [st] as the final or medial sound

Stahl	*steel*	**Ast**	*branch*
still	*quiet*	**ist**	*is*
Stein	*stone*	**einst**	*formerly*
Stuhl	*chair*	**Wurst**	*sausage*
stehen	*to stand*	**erst**	*first*
verstehen	*to understand*	**gestern**	*yesterday*
Einstein	*scientist*	**meistens**	*mostly*
anstoßen	*to toast* (in drinking)	**Ostern**	*Easter*
(du) **störst**	*you disturb*	(du) **hörst**	*you hear*
bestellen	*to order*	**erstens**	*firstly*

8 German **st** [ʃt] versus English **st** [st]

still	*quiet*		**still**
Star	*starling*		**star**
Staat	*state*		**state**
Stier	*ox*		**steer**
Straße	*street*		**street**
Stern	*star*	*he is*	**stern**
Stahl	*steel*		**steel**
Stiel	*stem*	*to*	**steal**
Stuhl	*chair*		**stool**
Stoff	*cloth*	*to*	**stuff**
stinken	*to stink*	*to*	**stink**
stricken	*to knit*	*he was*	**stricken**
Strom	*current*		**stream**
stehlen	*to steal*		**steal**
(er) hat **gestohlen**	*he stole*	*he*	**stole**
(er) **stand**	*he stood*	*he*	**stood**
(es) **steht**	*it stands*	*a*	**state**
er ist **stark**	*he is strong*	*the* **stark** *truth*	
stabil	*stable*		**stable**

9 German **sp** [ʃp] as the initial sound of a word or syllable versus German **sp** [sp] as the final or medial sound

Spaten	*spade*	**Aspirin**	*aspirin*
springen	*to jump*	**Inspiration**	*inspiration*

Beispiel	example	Wespe	wasp
abspringen	to jump off	lispeln	to lisp

10 German sp [ʃp] versus English sp [sp]

Spaten	spade	spade
spielen	to play	spill
Spaß	fun	speed
Spule	spool	spool
Sport	sport	sport
Speck	bacon	speck
Spiel	game	spiel (U.S. slang)
Spiritus	alcohol	spiritous
Split	gravel	split
Spott	mockery	spot
verspotten	to mock	spot
Spur	track	spur
spring!	jump!	spring
es ist spitz	it is sharp	splits
spinnen	to spin	spin
entspannen	to relax	span
spät	late	spade

11 German s as a voiced sound [š] versus ss, ß as an unvoiced sound [s]

reisen	to travel	reißen	to tear
Rose	rose	Rosse	horses
heiser	hoarse	heißer	hotter
laß!	leave it!	(ich) las	I read
Gase	gases	Gasse	narrow street
Hasen	rabbits	hassen	to hate
Rasen	lawn	Rassen	races
Riese	giant	Risse	cracks

12 German f [f] versus German v [f], pronounced the same way (except in most words of foreign origin)

fallen	to fall	Vater	father
Ofen	oven	von	from
offen	open	voll	full
hoffen	to hope	Beethoven	composer
feilen	to file	Veilchen	violet

fertig	ready	verlieren	to lose
Ferien	vacation	Verein	club
Efeu	ivy	vier	four
Frevel	sin	Vieh	cattle
Ferse	heel	Vers	stanza

13 Contrasting the spellings w [v] and v [v], pronounced the same way

wann	when	Vanille	vanilla
wer	who	Verb	verb
Wille	will	Villa	villa
Wasser	water	Vassall	vassal
wen	who	Venus	Venus

14 Contrasting w [v] and f or v [f]

Wall	wall	Fall	fall
Wolke	cloud	(dem) Volke	to the people
Wort	word	fort	away
Wetter	weather	Vetter	nephew
wir	we	vier	four
Wälder	forests	Felder	fields
Waden	calf of the leg	Faden	thread

15 Contrasting z, tz [ts] and s [š] in the same word

Tanzsaal	dance hall
Salzsack	salt bag
Schwarzseher	pessimist
Holzsäge	wood saw
Jazzsänger	jazz singer
rechtsseitig	on the right side
blitzsauber	spic and span
Salzsäure	muriatic acid

16 German ng [ŋ] versus German nk [ŋk]

Zangen	pliers	zanken	to quarrel
Engel	angel	Enkel	grandchildren
singen	to sing	sinken	to sink
Wangen	cheeks	wanken	to hesitate

17 German ich-sound versus German ach-sound

ich-sound after front vowels

mich	me		schlecht	bad
das **Pech**	bad luck; tar		zeichnen	to draw
euch	you		dichten	to write poetry
riechen	to smell		nichts	nothing
die **Eiche**	oak tree		du **möchtest**	you would like
recht	right			

ach-sound after back vowels

der **Bach**	brook		das **Loch**	hole
die **Sache**	thing		doch	nevertheless
die **Nacht**	night		pochen	to knock
machen	to make		der **Koch**	cook
lachen	to laugh		hoch	high
das **Buch**	book		der **Bauch**	belly
die **Buche**	beech tree		tauchen	to dive
suchen	to search		auch	also
fluchen	to curse		er **raucht**	he smokes

ich-sound after consonants

München	Munich		bißchen	little bit
die **Milch**	milk		das **Fläschchen**	small bottle
das **Mädchen**	girl		durch	through
welcher	which		der **Storch**	stork

Pronounce the singular and plural forms in sequence.

das **Loch**, die **Löcher**	hole		das **Buch**, die **Bücher**	book
der **Spruch**, die **Sprüche**	saying		das **Dach**, die **Dächer**	roof
der **Bach**, die **Bäche**	brook		die **Tochter**, die **Töchter**	daughter
der **Bauch**, die **Bäuche**	belly		der **Brauch**, die **Bräuche**	custom

18 German v versus German w

der **Vetter**	nephew		das **Wetter**	weather
vier	four		wir	we
Herr **Veit**	Mr. Veit		weit	far
das **Vieh**	cattle		wie	how
vorüber	past		worüber	about what
Macht dem **Volke!**	Power to the People!		die **Wolke**	cloud
voran	ahead		woran	at, in what

VOWEL SOUNDS

19 German **ei** versus German **eu** and **aü**

die **Feier**	*celebration*	das **Feuer**	*fire*
nein	*no*	**neun**	*nine*
die **Eile**	*hurry*	die **Eule**	*owl*
ich **leite**	*I direct*	die **Leute**	*people*
die **Meise**	*titmouse*	die **Mäuse**	*mice*
leiten	*to direct*	**läuten**	*to ring a bell*
die **Eier**	*eggs*	**euer** Buch	*your book*
der **Eiter**	*pus*	das **Euter**	*udder*
leise	*softly*	die **Läuse**	*lice*

20 German **u** versus German **ü**

die **Mutter**	*mother*	die **Mütter**	*mothers*
ich **mußte**	*I had to*	ich **müßte**	*I should*
tuten	*to honk*	die **Tüten**	*paper bags*
er **fuhr**	*he traveled*	**für**	*for*
er **wurde**	*he became*	er **würde**	*he would*
die **Gute**	*the good one* (female)	die **Güte**	*goodness*
im **Zuge**	*in the train*	die **Züge**	*trains*

21 German **i** and **ie** versus German **ü**

SHORT

das **Gericht**	*court*	das **Gerücht**	*rumor*
die **Kiste**	*box*	die **Küste**	*coast*
das **Kissen**	*pillow*	**küssen**	*to kiss*
der **Mist**	*manure*	ihr **müßt**	*you have to*
Frau **Nisser**	*Mrs. Nisser*	Frau **Nüsser**	*Mrs. Nüsser*

LONG

das **Tier**	*animal*	die **Tür**	*door*
vier	*four*	**für**	*for*
liegen	*to lie down*	**lügen**	*to lie*
spielen	*to play*	**spülen**	*to rinse*
die **Biene**	*bee*	die **Bühne**	*stage*
Kiel	Germany city	**kühl**	*cool*

22 German o versus German ö

schon	*already*		schön	*beautiful*
die **Tochter**	*daughter*		die **Töchter**	*daughters*
er **konnte**	*he was able*		er **könnte**	*he could be able*
der **Ofen**	*oven*		die **Öfen**	*ovens*
der **Gote**	*the Goth*		**Goethe**	*(German poet)*
die **Toten**	*the deceased*		**töten**	*to kill*
ich **stoße**	*I push*		die **Stöße**	*blows*

23 German a versus German ä

sagen	*to say*		**sägen**	*to saw*
er **naht**	*he is approaching*		er **näht**	*he sews*
sie **hatten**	*they had*		sie **hätten**	*they would have*
ein **alter** Mann	*an old man*		er ist **älter**	*he is older*
wir **waren**	*we were*		wir **wären**	*we would be*
mahnen	*to warn*		die **Mähnen**	*manes*
die **Sage**	*legend*		die **Säge**	*saw*

24 Long u versus short u

LONG			SHORT	
er **sucht**	*he searches*		die **Sucht**	*addiction*
das **Mus**	*jam*		ich **muß**	*I must*
er **flucht**	*he curses*		die **Flucht**	*flight*
rußig	*sooty*		**russisch**	*Russian*
der **Ruhm**	*fame*		der **Rum**	*rum*
er **bucht** es	*he books it*		die **Bucht**	*bay*
auf dem **Stuhle**	*on the chair*		die **Stulle**	*sandwich*

25 Long i versus short i

LONG			SHORT	
bieten	*to offer*		**bitten**	*to request*
der **Schiefer**	*slate*		der **Schiffer**	*boatman*
du **liest**	*you read*		die **List**	*trick*
das **Lied**	*song*		er **litt**	*he suffered*
wir	*we*		das ist **wirr**	*that is confused*
der **Stil**	*style*		es ist **still**	*it is quiet*
die **Bienen**	*bees*		**binnen**	*within*

26 Long o versus short o

LONG		SHORT	
rote Blumen	*red flowers*	die Rotte	*gang*
ich wohne	*I inhabit, live*	die Wonne	*delight*
die Sohlen	*heels*	sollen	*to have to*
dem Sohne	*to the son*	die Sonne	*sun*
der Schoß	*lap*	ich schoß	*I shot*
der Ofen	*oven*	offen	*open*
der Schrot	*buckshot*	der Schrott	*scrap metal*

27 Long e versus short e

LONG		SHORT	
das Heer	*army*	der Herr	*gentleman*
beten	*to pray*	die Betten	*beds*
ich stehle	*I steal*	die Stelle	*place*
wen	*who*	wenn	*if, when*
die Speere	*spears*	die Sperre	*turnstile*
das Wesen	*being*	wessen	*whose*
den (accusative singular of der)		denn	*because*

28 Long a versus short a

LONG		SHORT	
der Staat	*state*	die Stadt	*city*
der Stahl	*steel*	der Stall	*stable*
er kam	*he came*	der Kamm	*comb*
raten	*to guess*	die Ratten	*rats*
die Maße	*measures, sizes*	die Masse	*the mass*
der Kahn	*boat*	ich kann	*I can*
die Wahl	*election*	der Wall	*wall*

29 Exercise on vowel sounds

[$\bar{a}$]	Long, back a sound	**Vater** *father*, **Wahl** *election*, **Saat** *seed*, **raten** *to guess*
[a]	Short, front a sound	**Hand** *hand*, **Ratten** *rats*, **Mann** *man*, **Gesang** *singing*
[$\bar{e}$]	Long, closed e sound	**leben** *to live*, **wen** *who*, **Meer** *ocean*, **mehr** *more*, **Ehre** *honor*
[$\bar{\varepsilon}$]	Long, open e sound	**Mädchen** *girl*, **Käse** *cheese*, **ähnlich** *similar*, **Äther** *ether*
[ε]	Short, open e sound	**Welt** *world*, **rennen** *to run*, **Sätze** *sentences*, **ändern** *to change*, **empfangen** *to receive*, **erklären** *to explain*

| [ə] | Short, unstressed e sound [schwa] | hatte *had,* gefallen *to please,* Hose *pants,* Gesetz *law,* kommen *to come,* Ufer *shore,* Menschen *people* |

30 Exercise on vowel sounds

[ī]	Long, closed i sound	wir *we,* Idee *idea,* Juni *June,* Bier *beer,* Liebe *love,* hier *here,* ihr *they,* Vieh *cattle,* Bibel *Bible*
[I]	Short, open i sound	bitten *to request,* singen *to sing,* Lehrerin *teacher,* Gift *poison,* Film *movie,* Spinne *spider,* Gefängnis *prison,* ich *I,* billig *cheap*
[ō]	Long, closed o sound	wo *where,* Ofen *oven,* Philosoph *philosopher,* wohnen *to live,* Kohle *coal,* Boot *boat,* rot *red,* Obst *fruit*
[ɔ]	Short, open o sound	offen *open,* Sonne *sun,* von *from,* Sorge *worry,* Wolle *wool,* Dorf *village,* Post *mail,* Koffer *suitcase,* voll *full,* folgen *to follow,* Zoll *customs*

31 Exercise on vowel sounds

[ū]	Long, closed u sound	rufen *to call,* Fuß *foot,* Schuh *shoe,* gut *good,* Kuchen *cake,* Kuh *cow,* Huhn *chicken,* Geburt *birth*
[ᴗ]	Short, open u sound	Mutter *mother,* Luft *air,* Bus *bus,* null *zero,* Stunde *hour,* dumm *stupid,* gesund *healthy,* hundert *hundred*
[ȫ]	Long, closed ö sound	hören *to hear,* Söhne *sons,* Goethe *(poet),* schön *nice,* Öl *oil,* gewöhnlich *usually,* Österreich *Austria*
[œ]	Short, open ö sound	Löffel *spoon,* zwölf *twelve,* Wörter *words,* plötzlich *suddenly,* öfter *frequently,* Köln *Cologne,* Töchter *daughters,* können *to be able to*
[ȳ]	Long, closed ü sound	Tür *door,* Lüge *lie,* früh *early,* müde *tired,* typisch *typical,* süß *sweet,* führen *to lead,* fühlen *to feel,* Hügel *hill,* zynisch *cynical,* gemütlich *cozy*
[Y]	Short, open ü sound	müssen *to have to,* wünschen *to wish,* fünf *five,* pünktlich *punctually,* Gymnastik *gymnastics,* Hymne *hymn*
[y]	Short, closed ü sound [unaccented]	synonym *synonym,* Physik *physics,* Büro *office*

32 Exercise on vowel sounds

| [aɔ] | Diphthong au sound | Haus *house,* laufen *to run,* Mauer *wall,* Baum *tree,* Auge *eye,* Pause *pause,* kaum *hardly,* Couch *couch* |
| [ɔI] | Diphthong eu sound | Leute *people,* deutsch *German,* feucht *humid,* Mäuse *mice,* läuten *to ring,* Teufel *devil,* Räuber *robber,* heute *today* |

[ɑI]   Diphthong **ei** sound   **zwei** *two,* **leider** *unfortunately,* **reich** *rich,* **Stein** *stone,* **Mai** *May,* **Kaiser** *emperor,* **Bayer** *Bavarian*